BACKBONE

BACKBONE

by
MICHAEL
ROSEN

FABER AND FABER
24 Russell Square
London

First published in 1968
by Faber and Faber Limited
24 Russell Square London WC1
Printed in Great Britain by
The Bowering Press Plymouth
All rights reserved

SBN 571 08866 X

The first public West End performance was given at the Royal Court Theatre on May 8th 1968, with the following cast:

MALCOLM LEVIN	Ray Brooks
MARTIN LEVIN	Roy Holder
HARRY LEVIN	Harry Towb
PEG LEVIN	Thelma Whiteley
TANIA FORBES	Marty Cruikshank
ROBERT FORBES	Timothy Carlton
MR. FORBES	Edward Jewesbury
MRS. FORBES	Clare Kelly
JIM	Tom Chadbon
CAROLINE	Deborah Norton
POLICEMAN	Harry Meacher

Directed by: Bill Bryden

The original production of *Backbone* was given at the Playhouse Oxford by the Oxford University Experimental Club on November 13th 1967, with the following cast:

MALCOLM LEVIN	Richard Heffer
MARTIN LEVIN	Jules Boardman
HARRY LEVIN	Donald Macintyre
PEG LEVIN	Frances Hazelton
TANIA FORBES	Hermione Lee
ROBERT FORBES	Barry Hammett
MR. FORBES	Ian Lancaster
MRS. FORBES	Jenny Crowther
JIM	Chris Purnell
CAROLINE	Tessa Lawrence
POLICEMAN	Peter Irvin

Directed by: Christopher Honer

AUTHOR'S NOTE

There seem to be two main problems about staging this play:

(i) *Length*. This can be simply resolved by cutting it. The Royal Court cut Act Two, Scene Seven.

(ii) *The change of location*. Any heavy realistic paraphernalia designed to show the details of middle-class or digs living will only slow the play down and some very simple indication that there is a change is all that's needed.

ACT ONE

Scene One

The play opens at the Forbes's during a film slide show. On stage are all the Forbes, plus MALCOLM *who is visiting the house for either the first or second time. The slides that are being shown are visible to the audience.* MR *operates the projector while* MRS *sits in a dominant position in the room delivering what commentary there is. The first slide that is shown is a straight one of the sea. No details—just the sea with a small amount of beach.*

MRS: No, don't show that one, dear. That was just to finish the film.

ROBERT: Where was that then?

MRS: That's the bay you have to——

TANIA: What's the next one?

MR. I'm sorry the, er, damn—that's got it.

MRS: (*half whisper to* TANIA): I do wish you wouldn't interrupt. (MR *slides the next one across but it is upside down—as he is a fairly experienced handler of the machine it only whisks into sight for a split second. There is silence while he changes it. It is a picture of Tania when she was quite a bit younger.*)

TANIA: Oh, no, please.

MRS: Now you've got it round the wrong way, haven't you?

TANIA: No, I used to have my parting on the other side or something.

MRS (*to* MALCOLM): Well, she doesn't look much like that now. I'll never forget the fuss we had about buying that pullover. How it had to be the right collar and the right cuffs. Five guineas at Jaeger. Still it was your birthday, wasn't it, dear?

MR: I think she looks quite nice there.

TANIA: No more.

MRS: You have got a funny look on your face.
    (*Slide.*)
    It's that poky little chin of yours, isn't it? (*Laugh.*)
    (*Pause.*)

MR: Next?

9

MRS: I was just wondering whether we can show Malcolm the one of the bird sanctuary—I'm sure he'd be interested in that one.

ROBERT: Next.

MR: Well, I'll show what's next in the box, my dear.

MRS: Is anyone cold or am I imagining things?

(*No reply.*)

(*Silence while he changes it. This time it is a picture of the dog. A big, heavy, nondescript dog.*)

MRS: I think that's easily our best picture of Josie.

MR: Yes, I'm inclined to think it is.

MALCOLM (*sudden*): Good Lord! I'm terribly sorry, Mrs Forbes, but I'm afraid I must go. I hadn't realized it was so late. I have a connection at Baker Street at 11.15. I'm terribly sorry, I just hadn't realized that it was . . .

(*He peters out. General mood of uneasiness aided by* MRS *sounding slightly put out. Put-out noises, etc.*

MALCOLM *gets up, as does* TANIA *and* MRS, *still in the dark. The heads loom large on the screen and keep bumping into each other.*)

ROBERT: Well, put on the lights then.

MR: I'm sorry, the projector is, er, connected.

MRS: You'll see Malcolm out, will you, Tania dear?

MALCOLM: I'm terribly sorry about this, Mrs Forbes—I had no idea that it was . . .

MRS: That's all right—Hurry or you'll miss that train—they go at eleven past, twenty-six past, and so on past the hour—the one you'll get—have you got your bag?

MALCOLM: Thanks very much, Mrs Forbes—It's been a very nice evening indeed.

MRS: Well, do come again. Did you take your—ah, you have the exact time there—I'm afraid we're all a bit fast here to get daddy off in the morning—put the hall light on would you, Tania?—You will be cold waiting around on that platform won't you?—anyway—yes—we'll be seeing you——

(*All this time* MALCOLM *has been making obliging noises.*

MALCOLM *exits slowly and backwards.*)

MRS: Can you see all right? Daddy will fix the other light some time. What is the time? (*Out through the door.*) Malcolm's coat is on the first hook, isn't it, dear? No, the second.

MALCOLM (*off stage*): Well, goodbye everyone, then. Er, thanks.

    (*A few mutters within. Pause in the dark on stage.*)

MRS: Well, connect up the light, would you, Robert—there's not much point in going on, is there?

ROBERT: No.

    (*He does so to the sound of offstage mumbles from the parting* MALCOLM *and* TANIA.)

MRS (*gets up*): Extraordinary—why doesn't he go if he's in such a hurry.

    (*Door slams. Enter* TANIA *to yet more on-stage silence.*)

    The trains are always early. You have to get there at least five minutes before . . .

    (TANIA *sits down, goes to eat an orange. Checks herself. Is aware that she is being sort of watched—slight unease, then*)

TANIA: I'm going to bed.

MRS: About time, too. You haven't been in before twelve all week.

TANIA: Mum, I've told you I'm working.

MRS: I don't see why you can't get home of an evening. As——

MR: I should go to bed if I were you, my dear, you're probably very tired. (*Friendly.*)

ROBERT (*laughs, muttering*): Working with her wandering around like a randy chicken.

TANIA: Goodnight, Dad.

    (*Kisses.*)

MRS: You won't be able to get up in the morning. The trouble we have in getting you to get out of that bed in the morning. You always look so tired—if only you had a little more commonsen——

TANIA: Oh, hell. (*Walks out.*)

MRS: And switch the immersion off, will you, dear?

    (*Silence. Two people begin to speak at the same time.* MRS *gains precedence.*)

    You ought to go to bed yourself, you know. You're working tomorrow, aren't you? It's your——

ROBERT: If I get there.

MRS: What's come over you, then? One day you get to that office and say what a marvellous day it's been and the next you don't want to go near it. I don't understand why people can't get on with a job.

ROBERT: Oh, well, I'm going up then. Cut me some flowers tomorrow, would you. I want to give some to Caroline for her birth——

MRS: Caroline Marsh? (*Slight edge.*)

ROBERT: It's just that it's her birthday, that's all.

MRS. Yes, yes.

ROBERT: Anyway, a few flowers never did anyone any harm, did they?

MRS: No, no. Of course not.

ROBERT: O.K. Well, goodnight.

MRS: Goodnight, Robert, dear. (*To dozing* MR.) Robert's going to bed.
(*Exit Robert.*)

MR: Goodnight, Rob.
(*Long pause.*)

MRS: Well, we might just as well be going up ourselves. Are you working early tomorrow?

MR: Yes.

MRS: I see, I shall be on my own again this weekend.

MR: Mmmm. (*Pause.*) You know one of the curious things about that projector is that no matter how often—Tania does look nice in that photo with the——

MRS: By the way. I haven't done the beds yet. I did the children's and mine when the bob-a-job came and I clean forgot.
(*Pause.*) I suppose you could call it wavy but it's sort of frizzy, isn't it?

MR: Mmm?

MRS: His hair.

MR: Yes, it is.

MRS. I don't suppose you noticed.

MR: No, I didn't. Mmmm.

MRS (*Calling out and exits*): Josie. Josie. Josie.

Scene Two

On stage are MALCOLM *and* JIM, *working in the lab. Knocks at the door after thirty seconds of them working and muttering to each other,* 'Come and have a look at this,' *etc.*

MALCOLM (*preoccupied*): Hello.
 (*Enter* TANIA.)
 Oh——

JIM: Hello, Tania.

TANIA: Hello. (*Slight uneasiness.*)

JIM: Oh, well. Evacuate.

MALCOLM: No need to go, Jim.

JIM: Oh, might as well. (*Mumble-mumble—slight begrudgement.*) Every dinner hour, etc., etc. (MALCOLM *watches him fixedly. Exit him.*)

MALCOLM: You don't have to knock, you know. (*To* TANIA.)

TANIA: You might have been . . . (*grails off*).

MALCOLM: I might have been what?

TANIA: I don't know.

MALCOLM (*contempt*): Busy.

TANIA: Yes.

MALCOLM: I'm never 'busy'.

TANIA (*taking a shade too literally*): Sometimes you are.

MALCOLM: Oh, yes. Sometimes I give the illusion that somewhere in a corner beneath a heap of specimens and file paper, I'm extending the domain of the understood. A total bloody waste of time.

TANIA (*slight pause. Watches him.*): But you know the only reason why I do any work now is that later—no—I'm going to say something silly.

MALCOLM: Never mind. It'll give me something to mull over all afternoon.

TANIA: I know. (*Obvious deflate.*)

MALCOLM: No, don't start that. (*Not unfriendly.*)

TANIA: I'm hungry. I didn't have any dinner—I don't know what I'm going to do next year.

MALCOLM: Oh, you'll run round in little circles like the rest of us—kidding yourself you're breaking down the frontiers of science in some obscure, squalid little area of unwanted fact. (*Enjoys it.*)

TANIA: I said I was hungry. (*Her kind of joke.*)

MALCOLM: I looked through every single ad. today. Khartoum. The University of Khartoum wants some grubbing little research assistant. Khartoum. Where is it? Kuwait? The Yemen? Be like living on a beach. Still. I'll apply and tell them I want to make documentary films of sand yacht safaris in the Sahara.

TANIA: You know Czeznic, or however you pronounce it?

MALCOLM: Sort of.

TANIA: He's, well, what do you think of him?

MALCOLM: What do *you* think of him?

TANIA: I don't know, really—he's all right, isn't he?

MALCOLM: No, he's a runt. A prize academic runt.

TANIA: Why?

MALCOLM: He might just as well be a bank manager. Next time you see him, tell him to polish his—well, he is, isn't he? (*He has noticed* TANIA *sort of switching off.*)

TANIA: Mmm—what time are you going back up?

MALCOLM: Oooo. I don't know. Depends whether there's anything here to distract me.

TANIA: Oh.

MALCOLM: Well, go on then.

TANIA: What?

MALCOLM: Distract me, for Christ's sake.

TANIA: How do I do that?

MALCOLM: We-e-ll——(*Mock thoughtful.*)

TANIA (*polite*): Do you like what you're doing?

MALCOLM: By and large: no. Are you feeling nervy or something?

TANIA: Why, what have I said?

MALCOLM: No, no, nothing . . . you sound a bit—well, anyway. (*Stops, tries again.*) They say when you start on all this, don't they, that all the really great discoveries have sprung from some very simple—well, Newton and his bleeding apple and Einstein and his braces or whatever. What gets me is that somehow the whole natural world is supposed to be *teeming* with simple ideas and I haven't got one.

TANIA: You'll be all right. I don't know what you worry about. I'm not even going to get a degree if I don't get on.

MALCOLM: What do you mean? That's all you do 'Get on'.

TANIA: Well, I want to get a——

MALCOLM: Good degree. Yes, yes, and so you shall.

TANIA: Well. Is that so bad?

MALCOLM: No, no. No, no. You slog away at it. Don't question if, just do it. That's what they want.

TANIA: Oh, come off it. I'm not as bad as those—as that lot in the second group.

MALCOLM: Oh, yes. The fervid girlies.

TANIA: Yes.

MALCOLM: Yes. In the first year great surging bands of dollies spill out into the corridors—everyone of then armed to the teeth with all the trappings and hardware of Britain's blithering little boutiques. One load starts revising for Armageddon the second week they get here and never stop.

TANIA: That's me.

MALCOLM: And there's the gang who spend half their time spraying you with their independence and sexual aloofness and before you know where you are, they've rushed off to the Continent and got screwed by a Greek taxi-driver or a Portuguese man-of-war or —well, whatever it is they all seem to need blokes in general far far more than any bloke ever wants them in particular.

TANIA: And what about——

MALCOLM (*pert*): It's their shoes. No bloke in a normal state of mind cares a halfpenny bugger what shoes a girl wears—but they strap themselves into Victorian ballet pumps and luminous baseball boots or these pre-war bulldozers smothered in purple candle wax. Purple. One year they will all suffocate themselves with bloody purple and the next they surge up the biochemistry lab steps blocked up to the eyeballs in lilac or canary or——

TANIA: Oh, well—that's me as well.

MALCOLM: Well, it keeps their minds off sex. Ironically enough.

TANIA: I don't think it matters. Everyone makes such a fuss and nonsense about what people look like. It doesn't matter.

MALCOLM: It's not me that's making it matter. It's the——

TANIA: Oh, yes, yes, yes. And look at you. (*Bright.*)

MALCOLM: Yes. (*Does so.*)

TANIA: Well?

MALCOLM: Not so bad, is it?

TANIA: You look like a lorry driver.

MALCOLM (*arms in the air*): 'Rough hewn lyricism.' See?

TANIA: No. (*Shuts eyes.*)

MALCOLM (*puts arm round her*): Come over here and have a look.

TANIA: No, I won't. (*Giggle.*)

MALCOLM: Come here and see. Open your eyes. (*Struggles. Succeeds —kisses.*)

TANIA: That's nice, I like that.

MALCOLM (*quick one again. Presses her nose with amazed curiosity*): God, you've got a rubbery nose. Incredible. Look at it. (*Presses more.*) I don't think I could ever have seen a nose quite like it. (*Presses. Makes a lot of it.*)

TANIA: Don't. (*Gets out hanky and starts age-long nose blowing, wiping, etc.*)

MALCOLM (*suffers in silence, watching the cleaning procedure with amazement, until finally*): Whatever else you might want to do, for God's sake blow your nose.

TANIA: What do your parents think of me.

MALCOLM: We're not going to have——

TANIA: No, tell me.

MALCOLM (*ratty*): I don't know.

TANIA: You know what mine think about you.

MALCOLM (*mock worry*): They think I'm a communist spy.

TANIA: I wanted to talk about this seriously.

MALCOLM: I didn't. (*Pause.*)

TANIA: That's my dinner hour nearly gone.

MALCOLM: Why are you a solemn sod?

TANIA: I'm not.

MALCOLM: Sorry, I was lying. (*Deadpan. Pause. Shouts*): And don't laugh. God, you're a gag a minute. (*Silence.*) What's the matter now? (*Mock long face.*) I am suffering in silence—I am

16

ignoring him because he is big and noisy—I am trying to
find something to suffer about as this is an important facet to
my contemplative personality.
(*She laughs.*)
Is anything the matter, Tania?—No—Is anything the matter,
Tania?—No— Is anything the matter, Tania?—No—Is
anything the matter, Tania?—We-ell——

TANIA: Oh, stoppit, Malc. Please. (*In control.*)

MALCOLM: Yes, Tania. (*Like 'Yes, sir.'*)

TANIA: Are you going to stay with me?

MALCOLM: You've survived it for a month.

TANIA: Why do you say——

MALCOLM: And why do you always want a running commentary
on everything we do?

TANIA (*oblivious*): You've been going out with me for a month.
That either means that you thought that I was nice to start
with and it's just beginning to dawn on you what a weed
I am, or you thought it'd be all right for a bit of a laugh and
now it's me who's laughing because you're still here.

MALCOLM: What *is* all this for? (*Amazed.*)

TANIA: I think you'll get fed up. That's an admission of weakness.

MALCOLM (*reasoning*): Don't turn it into a horoscope, love. You
don't affect the issue by making Gypsy Lee predictions
every time we see each other. Just try and BE, will you.
Just BE.

TANIA: But why do you get so angry? Why do you shout at me?
(*Curious, rather than moany.*)

MALCOLM: When was the last time I shouted at you?

TANIA: Yesterday.

MALCOLM: Why, what was I saying?

TANIA: (*realizing the daftness of it*): You said I was a twitchy,
tea-drinking cabbage.

MALCOLM (*half-laughing*): Jesu, joy of——yes.

TANIA: Why are you so violent about everything? Why do you
always shout?

MALCOLM: I shouted because I was exasperated. I was exasperated
because, because you're a big girl now. You shouldn't even
be LIVING at home, let alone having stinking tea there.

TANIA: Well, I haven't been around like you have.

MALCOLM: All I'm saying is that——

TANIA: And give me a gun and I'll go home and shoot my parents for you. Is that what you want? (*Annoyed.*) Everything's easy.

MALCOLM: I'm happy with you all right. Somewhere along the road of speedy promiscuous living you got left behind. And that's the way I like it. (*Mock sex.*)

TANIA: There's no point in you staying though, is there?

MALCOLM: No, none whatsoever.

TANIA (*a bit more desperate*): I'm still at home in everything.

MALCOLM: I'm bored now.

TANIA: And that I don't want to sleep with you yet?

MALCOLM (*getting a grip*): Hey—look you—doughy—if you thought I was in this game just for the bunk-up I wouldn't have lasted the month, would I?

TANIA: And what about the other girls?

MALCOLM: What about them?

TANIA: You slept with them?

MALCOLM: Yes. Well?

TANIA: That means you want to with me.

MALCOLM: Yes. Well? (*Identical intonation to the previous 'Yes. Well?'*)

TANIA: You do. I knew it.

MALCOLM: What do you mean, you knew it? I wouldn't have lasted this long if I didn't.

TANIA: Well, how long are you going to wait?

(MALCOLM *glances at watch.*)

TANIA: Tell me about the other girls. And tell me—tell me what it'll be like. I need convincing, Malc. I don't know——

MALCOLM: Tania, the other girls drove me mad—all two of them.

TANIA: And the others?

MALCOLM: Oh, yes—Land Rover Levin—goes anywhere—I don't count others. I went out with those two for two years each and both of them went grisly at the end.

TANIA: How?

MALCOLM: Both of them in exactly the same way: a month of feeble little bickering and whimpering—an announcement on her part that she felt that her independence was being

18

undermined and me tearing off after someone else. Both times resulting in a night of complete agony of tears and screams in their homes while their parents were away. Twice I had—oh, all night—it was—no.

ANIA: And did you love them?—Oh (*smiles*) I mean often.

MALCOLM: They decided that having committed themselves totally —they had missed seeing life. So I told them to bugger off and see life. With the rest of them. (*Picking up* TANIA's *last words.*) Yes, often. All the time. Dinner hours as well.

ANIA: Alice said——

MALCOLM (*yell*): Bloody Alice! Christ, that girl. Hello, men. Don't touch me.

ANIA: It's all right. I don't like her, either. I was only saying what she said.

MALCOLM: No, no. You take everything some sexual crocodile like her says, as some reflection on you.

TANIA: I hate Alice.

MALCOLM: That's what I mean.

TANIA: I don't want to be like her. I never have. It's——

MALCOLM: You probably know the circumference of her thigh.

TANIA: Look, I've never——

MALCOLM: Just try and do what *you* want to do not what the hordes do.

TANIA: I do, I do. I promise you. And all it does is isolate me one way or another.

MALCOLM: And so it should.

TANIA: And you haven't convinced me yet.

MALCOLM: What of?

TANIA: 'Bedding me', as you'd say. Go on. I need reassuring. It all seems like painful gymnastics to me. (*Her kind of joke.*)

MALCOLM: Well—I don't know. (*Self-conscious.*) It's very nice. Well, it *can* be——

TANIA: But how? How nice?

MALCOLM: Floating nice. Look——

TANIA: No. How, Malc?

MALCOLM: I say floating. I don't know. Dandelions.

TANIA: Have you ever said that to anyone else?

MALCOLM (*tired*): Actually it's my little seduction special. Last week it was sycamore seeds and the week before it was the broad bean.

TANIA: I'm sorry—I've spoilt it now—I've spoilt it. I always do, don't I? Why am I so——

(MALCOLM *quietens down* TANIA.)

TANIA: Look after me then.

(*He kisses her.*)

MALCOLM: Haven't you got a seminar or something now? (*Ironic.*) Something terribly vital anyway.

TANIA: Yes. Yes.

(*Detaches herself—he grabs her back.*)

Meet me at four outside the tube station and we'll spend the evening together in your digs. You can cook me a meal. You can cook me a meal, you can tell me a story, and you can seduce me like the dirty old man you are. (*Nervy concession.*)

MALCOLM: Bye then, love. Look after that bit, will you. (*Pointing to side of neck and touching it.*)

Scene Three

The next scene is in the Levins's House. HARRY *stands at the entrance to the kitchen talking to* PEG *offstage in the kitchen.*

HARRY (*grittily genial*): I don't think Martin's done a stroke of work all week—you know that? 'A' levels —you'd think he'd never sat an exam in his life the way he goes on. The minimum. The absolute minimum. I've never known anyone like him. (*Mutter, mutter.*) I don't know. A lifelong 'O' level oaf he'll be.

PEG: He gets along all right.

HARRY: And that's about it.

PEG: So did you.

HARRY: Did I? Like hell I did. Who was it who used to say 'No, not tonight, I've got work to do?' For Martin it's 'Yes, please, *because* I've work to do.' Oh, it makes me sick the way he

20

goes on. He can't have read a book in years. I've spawned an oaf. A total oaf.

PEG: You worry yourself daft over it. Leave him to get on with it.

HARRY: Malcolm's coming back this weekend, isn't he?

PEG (*enters*): Yes, with Tania.

HARRY: Uh huh.—You've got flour on your face.

(*She goes to brush it off but only puts more on with her floury hands.*)

No. No. Come here. (*He brushes it off her face and pecks her on the cheek when he's done.*)

PEG: Did you collect the stuff from Kingham's.

HARRY: Oh, God—I completely forgot.

PEG: I can't do it all on my own, you know.

HARRY: No-one's saying you should. I'm sorry but I forgot.

PEG: I can't do it all myself, you know. It's shut when I go in the mornings, and——

HARRY (*sits down in chair and picks up newspaper*): Are we going to have this all weekend. Why don't you shut up moaning?

PEG: —on Fridays I haven't got the time to get it all.

HARRY: No one's saying you should do it, for God's sake. I will get it myself tomorrow when I do the shopping. O.K.?

PEG (*also sits with newspaper*): You'll forget.

HARRY (*leans over and dops her on the head with a newspaper*): I won't —and what's more your intelligence is showing (*referring to skirt being too high. Pause while both read.*) What do you make of this Toni tinni girl, then?

PEG (*not concentrating*): Sounds quite a responsible sort of girl.

HARRY: That's a fine bloody thing to say. It's the 'responsible' girls that give in their work: On time, Beautifully Presented and Completely Boring. 'Responsible'. Actually that's just what I feared she was. 'A responsible girl.'

PEG: All right, all right—but I think she's quite nice.

HARRY: Yes, I suppose so. Still, we're back on the commuter belt now. Hoo Ray.

PEG: You've not said anything to him about it, have you?

HARRY: You hope *I* didn't say anything. Who does all the interfering in this place?

PEG: Well, it's not me, I can tell you.

HARRY: Oh, yes—who was it then who described Malcolm's nurse friend to his face as a fat Swedish pudding?

PEG: Once. The one and only occasion that I've ever said anything

HARRY: Well, I've never said a word, I'm sure.

PEG: They read your opinion all over your face.

(*Enter* MARTIN, *jokey sixth-former, in school uniform greatly adapted—he is in fact looking a mess. Main motive in life: to enjoy himself.*)

MARTIN: Like the time when he said to Marie, 'If you can't find your bloody way home at this time of night, then you're just not fit for this world.' She had snivels all the way home after that one. (*Laughs.*)

HARRY (*not aggressive*): Hello, oaf.

MARTIN: The thing the old man forgets is that not all the birds that come here are brought home as prospective mates for life.
(*Kisses Peg.*)

HARRY: I have no doubt that you can rationalize away any of your flirtations.

PEG: Who's interfering now?

HARRY: I'm not. All I'm doing is making a general comment.

MARTIN: Come off it. You're both so concerned that us two end up with decent birds who we're going to have 'worthwhile stimulating' relationships with, that by the time you've fallen over yourselves doing this non-intervention stuff, your attitudes are as plain as hell.

HARRY: All right, Charlie boy, what's the score on the new one then?

MARTIN: Don't think I'm not dying to find out.

PEG: Well, you can change into something decent then.

MARTIN (*mock helpful*): Boiler suit?

HARRY (*pointing to* PEG *bending down over the other side of the room: back to* HARRY): Interesting expression your mother's got on her face this evening.

PEG (*annoyed*): It's not funny any more, Martin. No-one's laughing I'm ashamed to see you in the street these days and I live in dread that you'll come up and see me at work. Why can't you just try and make yourself——(*Continues complaint*) —we ask you to do very little.

MARTIN: What gets me is the amazing hypocrisy of it all! You spend half your time coming back from school saying how you've just met such and such a rebel and such and such a nonconformist and the rest of the time you're going on at me for not being respectable enough. It stinks.

HARRY: Just look at yourself. What's all this? (*Grabbing hair.*) You ... look like a Greek ponce. (*Sees neck.*) My God—Peg, come and have a look at this boy's neck. You could grow mangoes in that. You need a syringe, Jack.

PEG: We must decorate the bathroom white.

MARTIN: Yes.

HARRY: What do you mean, yes? When was the last time you went in there to know that it needed decorating——

PEG: You're both a pair of pigs.

(*They enjoy the argument. Meanwhile,* MALCOLM *and* TANIA *have just arrived.* MALCOLM *calls out 'Hallo' off stage before the last comment and* TANIA *enters just in time to hear it. There is a momentary air of embarrassment on the part of* HARRY *and* PEG *which* MARTIN *relishes, but* TANIA *doesn't know how to react to it.*)

TANIA: Hallo, Mrs Levin, Mr Levin, how are you?

PEG/HARRY: Hallo, Tania, how are you?

HARRY: Got a syringe?

TANIA: Fine thanks, and you?

HARRY: Not so bad, you know. How's the work going?

MARTIN: Christ!

TANIA: All right. I'm still on time with my revision schedule.

(*Enter* MALCOLM.)

MALCOLM: Hi, folks. That's my brother.

HARRY: Oh, haven't you met dirty Dick before? (*Mock introduction.*)

MALCOLM: No, she hasn't. He's worse, you see.

TANIA: Well——

PEG: How are you, then, have you eaten?

TANIA: Well, yes, we have really, haven't we?

MALCOLM: No. Buns is not food. It's a wonder you haven't got beri-beri. It's all she ever eats.

TANIA: Well, it's too late for you to start cooking now, Mrs Levin.

HARRY: Who said anything about cooking? You can do as much of that as you want here. (*Often plays jokes to* MARTIN, *who enjoys them.*)

PEG: Don't take any notice of him.

(*He sniffs and snorkels.*)

And stop that. We haven't eaten either and I thought you probably wouldn't have as well. I'll go and see to it now.

TANIA: Well, I can help.

HARRY: Berlimey. That's quick. Huh. See that? (*To* MARTIN.)

PEG: And the men do the washing up.

(*Exit* PEG *and* TANIA.)

MARTIN: Washing up for *men*.

MALCOLM: No, Mart, we're bored with that one.

HARRY (*to Martin*): Don't mention that—she was having one of her moans earlier.

MARTIN (*imitating* PEG): 'I stand by the sink all day long while all you men sit about talking. I have a job to do. I can't do everything.'

MALCOLM: How are you, then, Dad?

HARRY: I've got a bloody cold and—oh—too much work, too much work. I can't keep up with it.

MALCOLM (*phoney sincere*): Yes, happens to all of us, doesn't it, Malc?

MALCOLM: I've got my work cut out coping with *life* at the moment.

HARRY: Why, what's the matter with it?

MALCOLM: Oh, nothing.

MARTIN: No, come on, Malc, what's the news?

MALCOLM: No, no, it's only her mother, that's all.

HARRY: No, not another one.

MARTIN: Why, what's happened, Malc?

MALCOLM: No, it's the normal stuff but somehow it's worse when you're trying like mad to avoid treading on their toes in any way. The last thing I wanted to do was to offend them and the old bag.

HARRY: Why, what's happened? He talks in hieroglyphics.

(*Re* MALCOLM *to* MARTIN.)

MALCOLM: Nothing to my face. It all comes via Tania. Having discovered I don't carry an initialled briefcase in the rush-hour

24

every morning and night in order to do a clean, responsible job in a clean responsible office, the pressure is on.

HARRY: Why, what has she said?

MALCOLM: Oh, only puny stuff about being brusque or that didn't Tania *mind* that my jacket was worn. Mind?—when we went for our little Sunday suburban drive, she plonked the dog on it to slobber and honk all over it all afternoon.

HARRY: Well, you're not going to start getting hurt about that, are you?

MALCOLM: No, no. A year ago I'd have been pleased to know that you could annoy women like her with something so trivial. But it's different now. I don't——

MARTIN: I don't see that anything's do different. You do what——

MALCOLM: Well, I don't still believe that a hairy face is the answer to all our most pressing social questions. I've had enough of junior bum's status: choosing between buying clothes *or* records *or* going out; without some suburban prune to remind me of it. I'm a big boy now. You have enough problems trying to make a go of it—Oh, I don't know. The whole subject is imbued with sickening familiarity.

HARRY: So long as you know what you're taking on there, Malc.
    (*He looks across to* MARTIN *and shrugs.*)

MALCOLM: Yeah, I know. (*Break*). How about you, Mart?

MARTIN: Oh—we're on to the tinies now, Malc. Blind devotion from first-formers, you know.

HARRY: Quite mad.
    (*Enter* TANIA *and* PEG.)
    Here's grub.

MARTIN (*to* MALCOLM): Getting a bit?
    (MALCOLM *ignores*.)

HARRY (*about* TANIA): What *she* looking so glum about?

PEG: Don't you start on her. She's been telling me about home.

HARRY: Why, what's the matter with it?

TANIA: Mum mainly.

MALCOLM: There you are.

HARRY: The moment these two get here they purge themselves of mumphobias. Go where there's mum leastly. Quite simple. Everyone's growing mothers these days.

TANIA: It's not so easy as that, Mr Levin.

PEG: No, quite.

HARRY: What do you mean: '*No*—quite'—You walked out of your home easily enough.

PEG: That's different. And haven't you got a hanky? He's turning into such a dirty old man.

HARRY (*mutters*): No Mum. Anyway—I don't see what's so different.

(*There ensues rapid laying out of food carried out by all characters. The table is laid informally. Everyone serves themselves. No one waits for anyone else. Mood boisterous. Eating off knees.*)

HARRY (*starts eating ostentatiously first*): Don't wait for me, anyone.

MARTIN: Great! Gherkins.

MALCOLM: God, I've missed real food. It's been baked beans and Mars bars all week.

TANIA: What do you mean? I cooked you a meal on Thursday, didn't I?

HARRY: That's what he means.

TANIA: It was rissotto.

HARRY: Oh, God—rissotto. In my day it was called fish and chips.

PEG: Well, you're getting pilaff tonight.

TANIA: And liking it.

MARTIN: I'm starting on the rice.

PEG: But what about the salad?

MARTIN: I'm skipping the French bit tonight.

MALCOLM (*stirring up trouble*): Not the only time you skip the French, is it?

MARTIN (*mouths*): Yeah yeah.

TANIA: Can I have something to drink?

HARRY (*to* PEG): She's not supposed to ask.

PEG: Serve yourself, Tania.

HARRY: And blow the expense—daddy will pay.

TANIA: Does he?

HARRY: Always—that's the point.

MALCOLM: Good old daddy.

(*Sudden close of scene mid-dialogue.*)

Scene Four

Opens at dinner at the Forbes's with MALCOLM *and Robert's girl*
CAROLINE *present. Everyone is seated at the table except for* TANIA
and MRS. *The table is set, but as yet, bare of food. Few coughs,
drinking of water, passing of jug, unfolding of napkins, etc.—i.e.
obvious contrast with ending of previous scene.*

MRS: Will you bring in the peas, Tania?

TANIA (*offstage, entering*): I am. (*Edge of annoyance.*)

MRS: And don't forget the water jug—oh, no, there it is. Daddy
    will you carve or do you want to, Robert?

TANIA: Dad will.

MR (*quite unaware of Robert's keenness to impress*): I'm quite happy
    to.

ROBERT: Oh, go ahead, Dad.

MR: Right.

MRS: I'll serve the peas if you pass the plates up to me.

CAROLINE: I'll do the potatoes, then.

MRS: Would you?

CAROLINE (*opens dish*): Oh, they're lovely, Mrs Forbes.

MR (*having cut the first slice*): First one, then (*he passes it to* CAROLINE
    for the potatoes, who passes it on to MRS *for the veg, who then
    passes it on to* MALCOLM *who makes to offer it to* CAROLINE. *A
    knife falls off a plate and everyone jumps.*)

CAROLINE: No, no, I'll wait as I'm doing this.

MALCOLM (*awkwardly*): Oh, er, right.

MRS: Yes, you go ahead, would you, Malcolm?

MALCOLM: Fine, thanks very much. (*He goes to start, but checks
    himself.*)

    (*N.B. No one starts until everyone is served.*)

TANIA: Gravy? (*Helping him out of bother.*)

MALCOLM: Please.

MR: Next.

CAROLINE: Oh, the potatoes are super, Mrs Forbes.

MALCOLM: Very nice.

MRS: You take this, Tania dear.

TANIA: Thanks. (*Slight amount spilled.*)

MRS: That's a new tablecloth. Why are you so messy? Well, get a cloth then. Look at it. I don't—— (*very agitated*).
(*Exit and re-enter* TANIA *with the cloth.*)
Oh, look at it, etc.
(*Pause.*)

MR: Fine piece of meat, dear.

MRS: Yes, I should think so at the price.

MR: Very nice.

CAROLINE: Is that the butcher at the end of King's Street? Oh, he's a lovely man, isn't he?

ROBERT: Why?

MRS: Just try to be a bit more sensible, Tania.

CAROLINE: He has a lovely big red face.

MRS: No, I won't have any potatoes, thank you, Caroline.

ROBERT: That butcher's a swine.

MRS: Robert—really.

ROBERT: Well, he is. I remember when I was a kid, going in there and asking him what sausages were made of, and he said, 'Little boys. Now (*gestures*) clear off.'

MRS: I don't——

TANIA: Or like the time when we wanted some sawdust off him for stuffing the guy and he said there was only one thing he knew worth stuffing in the world, and laughed. I never knew what it meant. I always thought 'Get stuffed' had something to do with November after that. (*Her 'innocence' disguises her intentions.*)

MRS: Really, whenever we have visitors you two start up. (*Trying to brush it aside. Pause.*) Well, Malcolm, how are *you* getting on?

MALCOLM: Very well, thanks, Mrs Forbes.

MRS: How are all those rats you keep?

CAROLINE (*incredulous*): He doesn't.

MRS: It is rats?

MALCOLM: Yes, that's right—well—all fine, all fine.

MRS: Do you kill them yourself? (*Disapproving.*)

CAROLINE: Do you kill them?

MALCOLM: No, the lab staff do that.

TANIA: Tell them what you do with the female rats when they're on heat.

MALCOLM (*embarrassed*): No, look, I——

TANIA: Oh, I will then. He takes one of these female rats that are all sort of keen and drops her into a cage full of males, and watches what happens. They go berserk, don't they, Malc? They do. (*Complete silence.*)

ROBERT: Sounds quite a life you have up there.

MALCOLM: No, look——

TANIA: I think that's funny—don't you?

MRS: Yes, dear.

MR: Must be extraordinary to——

MRS: Well, Caroline, and what about you? What've you been up to since we last saw you?—which is a long time, isn't it? (*Doing the rounds.*)

CAROLINE: Yes, it is. Well—hard to think, really. Oh, yes, of course—I'm forgetting. Last week on Saturday, the boss's daughter got married, so all the girls from the office went along. We had all put in a little bit for them and it was enough to get them a coffee table and one of those nice leather folder-things you put the Radio Times in.

MRS. Sounds very nice.

CAROLINE: Oh, it was. It was marvellous. In the upstairs room of the Bedford Arms which was really very swish and everything.

MRS. Who's the groom, then. (*Participating.*)

CAROLINE: Oh, yes, I forgot to say, well it was quite a coincidence. HE'S DADDY'S BEST FRIEND'S SON. He's just finished doing insurance, and has just set himself up on his own. He is dishy. He had everybody laughing so much in his speech. I think she is jolly lucky to have got him, to tell the truth.

ROBERT: Like me.

CAROLINE: No, you're more sort of sweet, isn't he, Mrs Forbes?

MRS: Oh, yes, he's always been our sweet Robert, hasn't he, Tania?

TANIA: Yes.

(*Pause.*)

MRS: You know—I think there must be something wrong with Mrs T. these days: no matter when I see her, no matter what

29

time of day or night she's in her dressing-gown with all her hair all over the place. I think she——

TANIA: Probably an invalid——

MRS. No, I don't think so. I think she's just too lazy to get dressed properly. And she always looks fast asleep. She's got funny little squinty eyes that peep out at you like bats. I mean, they're a very odd pair, aren't they?

CAROLINE: *Do you* cut up animals?

MALCOLM: Well, you see—when we're trying to have a look at something that goes on inside then we have to——

CAROLINE: But that's awful, how could you?

TANIA: Why? You put them under anaesthetic, don't you, Malc?

MALCOLM: Yes, of course. And they're killed immediately afterwards.

MRS: Are they?

CAROLINE (*to* TANIA): I could never go around with someone with the blood of live animals on his hands (!)

TANIA: Doesn't worry me, actually. At least, it hasn't for the last three months so I don't see why it should in——

CAROLINE: Oh, it's that long, is it?

(MRS. *gets up.*)

TANIA: What?

CAROLINE: You.

MRS. Daddy, will you cut the rest of the meat—there are second helpings for some—who wants?

(*No one replies.*)

Malcolm—you must.

MALCOLM: Well, thank you very much. Really not.

MRS: Anyone else?

(*No one else.*)

Are you sure? I don't want to be left with any. Caroline—Daddy—Tania——

(*No one.*)

—Oh, dear. It must be finished—Malcolm, surely . . .

TANIA: Leave him alone, Mum.

MRS: I hate having any left over. Oh, well. We'll have the pie straight away then.

(*The plates are collected to accompanying dialogue:* 'Pass up
the plates,' etc.)

MRS: Very nice, etc., etc.

(MRS *serves the pie to general quiet apart from:* 'There's yours,
Tania—Robert,' etc., etc.)

MRS: Would you serve the custard, Tania? They're our own apples,
you know.

(*Pause.*)

CAROLINE: Oh, look at Robert—he eats his crust first and leaves
the juicy bit till last. I can never wait. I'm sure there must be
some psychological reason for that.

ROBERT: Yes—get the boring bit over first.

MALCOLM: Not like my brother who eats the whole lot at once.

(*Laughs.*)

MR: What, in one mouthful? (*Not amused—likes idea.*)

MALCOLM: Sort of.

MRS: Good Lord, what does your mother say?

MALCOLM: I think they've given up with him—besides he learnt all
his worst habits from my dad.

(*Laughs—silence.*)

CAROLINE (*quietly*): Could I have a touch more custard, please,
Mrs Forbes?

MRS: Yes, of course.

CAROLINE: Lovely.

(*Pause while everyone eats.*)

MRS: Well, what's happening this afternoon? Daddy's easy—he's—
having his nap. Robert and Caroline have promised to do
the lawn—how about you?

MALCOLM: Well, we could help with the washing up.

TANIA: Yes.

MRS: No, no, no. I'll do that. I've got nothing else to do this
afternoon. So what are you going to do?

TANIA: I don't know—read or something.

MRS: I see. Well, are you going to be about for tea?

TANIA: I don't know.

MRS: What do you mean, you don't know?

TANIA: Well, maybe we will or maybe we won't.

MRS: Well, make up your minds, then.

TANIA: But I don't know whether we'll want to go out.

MRS: I think the very least you could do is tell me whether to get tea for you.

TANIA: But we can get tea ourselves if we want it.

MRS: But there's no point in making everything dirty twice.

TANIA: Well, don't wash up then—we will.

MRS: Really, Tania, sometimes you just try to make things so difficult.

TANIA: I don't see why——

MR: All right, Tania, that's enough. (*Quiet and knowing.*)

MRS: Well, then, if someone will help me clear the table we will all get on.

(*Table is cleared,* ROBERT *and* CAROLINE *go out with a* 'Let's get on with the lawn, darling.' MALCOLM *and* TANIA *exit with* TANIA *in the lead mouthing disgust.* MRS *re-enters and talks to dozing* MR.)

MRS: Well, I really don't think Caroline need have been quite so blatant, do you?

MR: Mmm? (*Questioning grunt.*)

MRS: You'd never have thought that the engagement broke off a month ago—I can't see Robert sticking with her.
(*Exit* MRS.)

MR: Difficult to say, really.
(*Re-enter* MRS.)

MRS: Fancy Malcolm spending the whole meal talking about killing animals. When he started talking about opening those animals up, I felt . . .

MR: It must be quite an interesting sort of job for a young man like him. Tania's——

MRS: Where have they gone?

MR: Up to her room, I think.

MRS: Have they? I don't know what's come over Tania. All that about tea. She makes such a fuss over everything now—just a simple thing like coming to tea.

MR: Yes, dear.

MRS: Not that you ever seem to care. You'd make excuses for her if she robbed the bank of England, if I wasn't here. What is a

zoologist? What does he do with all these animals? Was the
lunch nice?

MR: Most enjoyable, dear.

MRS: Can you give me a little extra housekeeping this week—I want
to buy enough fertilizer for the whole bottom bed.

MR: I don't think I can get to the bank tomorrow, dear.

MRS: You always say that. I do the very best with what you give
me—I'd have thought that the least you could do was to help
me——

MR: I'm sorry but I really won't have time tomorrow.

MRS: Another one of your meetings, I suppose.

MR: No. dear.

MRS: Why don't you get one of those young men to do a thing
for a change?

MR: Yes.

MRS: Oh, well, I'd better get on with the washing up, I suppose. Is
Tania using the new fire? She never uses the old one.
(*Exit, leaving* MR *dozing.*)

Scene Five

TANIA's *bedroom.* TANIA *asleep in bed. Suddenly* MALCOLM *appears at
the door. He levers the door open and climbs in, stopping from time
to time to check that he hasn't been heard. As he comes into the room*
TANIA *wakes up.*

TANIA: What's that?

MALCOLM (*gets to her bedside*): Sh, sh, quiet, it's me, Malc.

TANIA: What? Why have you come? You can't come here.

MALCOLM: But I have.

TANIA: How did y——

MALCOLM: Along the corridor—squeaking boards as well—aren't
you glad to see me?

TANIA: Malc—why have you come? You're mad sometimes.
You're mad. You must have walked past their door.

MALCOLM: My bed was cold, the defendant said.

TANIA: But they'll hear you. You can't stay.

MALCOLM: Oh—that's nice.

TANIA: If they found us they'd throw us out immediately.

MALCOLM: Wouldn't do you any harm.

TANIA: I don't know what to say. Kiss me, you ape.

(*He does so.*)

I'm scared.

MALCOLM: Of them or me?

TANIA (*finally*): You can't come here now. I won't be able to face them in the morning.

MALCOLM: Why—what have *I* done? (*Nearly amazed*).

TANIA: I don't know. It could never be nice here. Oh, this is ghastly.

MALCOLM: But——

TANIA: Shh—what was that?

MALCOLM: Josie, Josie, Josie (*imitatively*).

TANIA: I don't want to lose you this way.

MALCOLM (*aggressive*): What?

TANIA: If it works—then it becomes a substitute, and if it doesn't then you leave. Either way everything else we do loses on it.

MALCOLM; Where did you learn that bit of virginal dogma?

TANIA: Oh, I don't know—make me want it.

MALCOLM (*heavy over-enunciation*): Want it.

TANIA: Why must it be here? You could have trapped me in your digs. You know what I want. I mean I don't know. Don't I?

MALCOLM: Are you going to throw me out now?

TANIA: When will you go?

MALCOLM: In the morning, if you haven't shot me before that.

TANIA: Daddy gets up at seven.

MALCOLM: More creepy crawlies at six then.

TANIA: I don't know, Malc.

MALCOLM: You wouldn't rather me stand in the cupboard all morning.

TANIA: I hate it here. You shouldn't have come.

MALCOLM: 'I shouldn't have come.' Better?

TANIA: It'll affect everything else.

MALCOLM (*gently*): Do as you want then, love. I can't force you.

(*Edge of tiredness*)

34

TANIA: You could seduce me. (*Pert.*)

MALCOLM: Could I?

TANIA: I don't know. Maybe.

MALCOLM: Can I come in now, then?

TANIA: Yes, yes—Don't frighten me, will you.

MALCOLM: No.

TANIA: That's when you say you love me. You don't do it right.

MALCOLM: I do, I do.

    (*Mutters.*)

ACT TWO

Scene One

TANIA *in bed at* MALCOLM'*s digs.* MALCOLM *has got up and is sitting at table. Notices* TANIA *after a bit. She is asleep. Moves in on her, grabs pillow and starts belting her with it while shouting.*

MALCOLM: Get up, get up, get up. You've got breakfast to make. Corn flakes to cook. Get up. The weekend. You'll never get to school on time. (*Mrs*) Do you want your pills, dear? (*Still belting her.* TANIA *begins to retaliate with the other pillow.*)

TANIA: Oh, you really are a big ape.
   (*They fight.*)

MALCOLM (*while fighting*): Well, what do you make of this round, Keith? Well, Eddy, I've seen some pretty savage, not to say fierce, onslaughts in my time but I reckon this one takes the biscuit. How about you, Eddy? (*The first was frenetic, this one, while holding* TANIA *down is very leisurely.*) Well, Keith, I've seen some pretty savage, not to say fierce, onslaughts in my time but I reckon this one takes the biscuit. That's how I see it, Keith. Thanks a lot, Eddy. (*He now lets her win.*) Ref, ref, ref. Come on then, get up, love. (*Kisses before and after last sentence.*)

TANIA: Do you give in?

MALCOLM: I always have.

TANIA: I do wish you'd behave.

MALCOLM (*hears something*): Sh, sh, sh. (*Whispers.*) Landlady. (*Goes to door to listen, comes back.*) O.K. Hitchcock over. Cuddly time. (*Quick cuddly.*)

TANIA: If you didn't make so much noise you'd never have to do that.

MALCOLM: No, dear.

TANIA: You always do though, don't you?

MALCOLM: Yes, dear.

TANIA: And put a kettle on.

MALCOLM: Yes, dear. (*Claps ear to wall.*) Not a squeak from old hot-rodding Lawson in there either. My turn. (*Bashes wall in mock coitus rhythm.*)

TANIA: What's he?

MALCOLM: A barbarian. Dandruff and a black shirt. Whistles Val Doonican in the bog.

TANIA: Malc?

MALCOLM: You know what I've decided: bed is vital in my life— no I don't mean with you. I just mean bed. There are some evenings I get back . . .

TANIA: The kettle, Malc.

(*She pushes the kettle against* MALCOLM'S *oblivious stomach while he's talking.*)

MALCOLM: There are some evenings I get back here and I climb into that bed as if it—no, I'm not going out there to fill the kettle —what do you think my bushranger's act was for? She'll whip in here to have a little talk the moment she hears the door open.

TANIA (*taking the kettle back*): You're intimidated by her.

MALCOLM: There's some water in the kettle anyway.

TANIA (*discovers that there is in fact no water in the kettle*): There isn't. (*Accepts the fact fairly good-naturedly.*) It's lovely coming here.

(*Look of boredom crosses* MALCOLM'S *face.*)

No, really, Malc. They're become like a refuge these weekends, you know. Do you tell anybody?

MALCOLM: (*Groan.*)

TANIA: Secret.

MALCOLM (*ironic plus stutter*): A-a-a-and ill-illicitly ssssexual.

TANIA: I couldn't live like you, you know.

MALCOLM: Well, don't.

TANIA: I could live with you, though.

MALCOLM: Maybe, maybe.

TANIA: I wouldn't want to sort of slide sideways into marriage, though.

MALCOLM: No, dear.

TANIA: You think I'm talking rubbish again.

MALCOLM: Yes, dear.

TANIA: Well, why don't you ever talk to *me*? Sometimes I think you don't really want to talk to me.

MALCOLM: True. What do you want to talk about?

TANIA: Anything. What did you do yesterday?

MALCOLM: Yesterday. Mmmm. Yesterday I arrived at the lab at ten o'clock—said hallo to everyone till eleven and then remembered I hadn't had any breakfast. I then quietly rigged myself up a bunsen, tripod and 500-mill flask, poured an estimated ten mills of white mice milk ration in; whipped across to the incubator; took out two large white eggs, only one day incubated; broke them into the flask and scrambled them. Though there was no——

TANIA: But they're fertile.

MALCOLM: I'm not fussy—a bit of embryo never did anyone any harm.

TANIA: That's revolting.

MALCOLM: Never mind the foetus—the tricky bit came when the prof walked in and there's me in the middle of the embryology research lab with the flask (*imitates frying noise*), eggshells all over the place—each one stamped 'zoo lab asterisk stroke one two bracket aitch.' 'Huh—morning, professor.' (*Smiling obliging.*) 'Morning, Mr Levin.'

TANIA: Mister?

MALCOLM: 'Morning, professor, hah' (*repeats frying noise*). 'Late breakfast, Mr Levin?'—'Late breakfast, professor.' 'Not so keen on lion eggs myself,' he says and walks out.

TANIA: He doesn't sound a bad bloke. I don't know why you always moan about him.

MALCOLM: He twitches. Shifty.

TANIA: All talented people twitch. Very bright people always have some little tic or other. You know if you didn't complain and dismiss people so much you'd be quite good at your work. Channel it all on to that.

MALCOLM: Should I?

TANIA: Well, there's an awful lot of energy gets lost.

MALCOLM: It's vital I spend three-quarters of my life spotting other people's insanities.

TANIA: Sometimes you must leave *me* alone, though.

MALCOLM (*turns to a mock audience—holds up mock microphone to either breast*): Well, how about that—and how do *you* two feel this morning?

TANIA: You know what Robert said?

MALCOLM: No—I don't know what bloody Robert said—and I don't want to know.

TANIA: I'm sorry. (*She isn't.*)

MALCOLM: What's sick about your brother is his way of talking about things: in cocky little formulae—'Yes—well—all people with superiority complexes have inferiority complexes too, you know.' He's the sort of bloke who gets up in the morning and puts his pants on in front of a mirror.
(*Knock at the door: Northern accent says:* 'Hallo, Malc; hallo, Malc.')

MALCOLM (*frantic*): Hang on, Jim, hang on, won't be a minute, hang on.

JIM: Can I borrow the scissors?

MALCOLM: Hang on. (*Gestures to* TANIA *to rustle the bed—whips off shirt, etc., to bare arm.*) Won't be a mo! (*Whispers to* TANIA.) Giggle. (*She does. Picks up scissors in bare hand—passes them out through the door so that only the naked arm shows.*)

JIM: Oh, sorry, Malc—I didn't realize—you were——

MALCOLM: That's all right, Jim, don't worry, eh? (*Accepting the apology with grace—forgivingly.*)
(*Door shuts—Pause.*)

TANIA: What was all that about?

MALCOLM: Why don't they all go off and burrow. This place. Jovial little Indians phoning all day about rocking chairs and the Korean lawyer upstairs banging ten-inch nails into his door all night, and the bog—the landlady has supplied a four-foot red broomstick to crank the cistern with because the ballcock sticks—a bloody mattress made of rhino hide and parsnips—cast iron chairs and the bathroom smells of dog slobber and Lawson's tarts. Old Jim up there can call his room a bed-sitter—he's only got the bed bit. Gets out of bed in the morning and falls out the door. They ought to advertise his room as a single bed-stander. Bed-sitter phuh! I want my own home now. I've had enough of trendy little pigsties.

TANIA: Maybe we will.

MALCOLM: And suddenly it was 'WE'...

TANIA: I like coming here.

MALCOLM: Even though you say sleeping with me is like sharing a bed with an old carpet.

TANIA: Well, it would be nice if you had a haircut. I cope. Having it off with an Axminster. (*Strokes his hair.*)

MALCOLM: You're turning into a right crude little bag, aren't you? (*In imitation of Landlady*): I don't know—don't talk to me about students—I've seen them.

TANIA: My, Mrs Roberts——

MALCOLM: She had a bit by—you know on one side like, and she did up her other place—all nice in pink and blue—it was real lovely it was—and she had the university people in and a month later hundreds of these students moved in. Hundreds of them. So big and dirty. And the mess they made——

TANIA: My, Mrs Roberts——

MALCOLM: She says—come over and have a look at this, she says. Oh, it was a crying shame it really was. The floor was all like dirty and scum and the sink—Oh, it breaks your heart, it really does.

TANIA: And they don't do any work, you know.

MALCOLM: And the bathroom—the bathroom, she says. Dust on the floor of a bathroom, she says. How can you have dust on the floor of a bathroom, she says. It's never used—that's why. You can't tell me anything about students.

TANIA: And the stories.

MALCOLM: You know what she told me; well, I don't know, she says—my husband—he's no teetotaller and I don't know why he should be—but these students. Every night. Every single night, she said.

TANIA: And they can't keep it down them.

MALCOLM: They're all so young. They're such youngsters.

TANIA: They can't keep it down them.

MALCOLM: And up it comes—all over the new wallpaper. It's peeled off upstairs, you know. Peeled right off the wall. It's a crying shame—it really is. And you know what—you know what—she says—she went to clean the sofa and she lifted off the

cushion thing—well, I'm a married woman, Mrs Jenkins, she
says. I'm a married woman—but down the back of the—
no, no. That's too much. I shan't let it out to students again,
she says.

TANIA: Maybe I was brought up different, she says.

MALCOLM: I'll have a nice quiet couple in—no children—not that
I've got anything against children mind. No dogs, no kids.
(*He begins to adopt his own voice.*) No zulus, no knives, no
forks, no bed linen—ah, it makes you sick—expand the
universities. (*Despair. Pause.*) What are we going to do this
weekend, then?

TANIA: I'll cook a really self-indulgent breakfast. Walk for miles
and miles and you're not going to complain that I'm having
a period.

MALCOLM: You timed it just right for the weekend. It's all right—
it's all part of my new thesis. Whenever anything
apparently logical but in fact totally ridiculous occurs—it
falls into the category of 'bum'. 'Bum' is world inverted.
Bum upwards. Most of the time *you* are 'bum'. Like my
mother during the Aberdeen typhoid epidemic a couple of
years ago. She goes to the cupboard—goes to take down a tin
of Fray Bentos and then says: 'Oh, dear no—we'd better not
open that until the typhoid outbreak's over.' Pure bum.

TANIA: Will you change the sheets?

MALCOLM: Soon, soon.

TANIA: Malc—am I nice? In bed, I mean, I suppose. I don't think
I know what it's about. (*Laughs.*) I can't stand the pace. I'll
have TB at thirty. Does it—does it matter about—I don't
know what it's really for yet. The end bit—Maybe—I'm not a
—Love me, will you.
(MALCOLM *then performs lecherous pawing act.*)
You know, you get really ratty if I don't want it, you know. It
annoys me—or scares me or—*stop that!* (*Pawing.*)

MALCOLM: We're just clearing away the brambles and barbed wire.

TANIA: Where from?

MALCOLM: Oooh. Any metaphorical path they might be blocking.

TANIA: I hadn't noticed them.

MALCOLM: That's what you're moaning about.

41

TANIA: I do moan, don't I? I disappoint you.

MALCOLM: But we had all that mid-week. 'Will we cut each other to pieces, Malc?'

TANIA: We will, I will. You know what happened Wednesday night. I went home—ran upstairs—put my head under the covers. I couldn't face seeing or doing anything. The work just batters me. My hands have come out in sympathetic spots. I've wasted three years by coming here. I don't know why I work. And then suddenly I can't stand it and I go and hide all on my own. The work—I can't, I can't say anything—it's just turkey gobble what I write down now. I just cried till my face ached. I can't work the way I used to. And I just cry instead. For hours.

MALCOLM: But you could——(*helpful gesture*).

TANIA: And decisions—you see this jam here (*in bag*), you know how long it took me to choose that? About half an hour. I stood looking at the counter paralysed—I couldn't choose between the black, cherry or the apricot—no, really, I couldn't—and then the moment I had bought it I felt terrible. About indulging myself. Clothes as well—I—I'm mentally ill about food. (*Getting agitated.*)

MALCOLM: Well, you can blame it onto that predatory crow of a mother you've got.

TANIA: That doesn't help. You've got to——(*breaks off in agitation.*)

MALCOLM: Yeah, yeah.

TANIA: Don't start looking like that. Everything sinks when you make that face.

MALCOLM: Come here——(*cuddles*).

TANIA: This weekend's going to be bad, Malc. I can't——(*edge of tears in her voice*).

MALCOLM: What you needed was a lovely bit of thump (*Kiss.*)

TANIA: Tomorrow. Tonight you can tell me one of those mad stories about your primary school sweetie-pies. I think I'm in danger of identifying with Valerie Bean. *I'd* have cried off if you'd said that about *my* cat.

MALCOLM: Come then—I'll dress you—say good morning to Thing Thong down there, andwe'll have a romp in the park.

Scene Two

Enter HARRY, *followed by* PEG *later.*

HARRY: Ordeal over. We've done our parental bit.

PEG: Make us some coffee, Martin.

MARTIN: No, hang on. What happened? What did old ma Forbes say when you walked in?

HARRY: No, no nothing. It's the usual. All very polite and nice from start to finish.

MARTIN (*insistent*): No, what was it like though? Are they as bad as Malc says?

HARRY: It's the usual stuff. She sits at home and——

MARTIN (*interrupting*): Hey—you never guess—incredible—you know I've been seeing them in town—well apparently, according to Tania—you'll never guess but——

HARRY: No I wouldn't guess. Any time you want to know what the Forbeses are like, ask your father—I don't know anything about it.

MARTIN: No, look. Hang on. Come on then. Tell your story first.

PEG: Coffee, Martin.

MARTIN: No, no. Look Dad, come on.

HARRY: Nothing to say.

MARTIN: Dad. Christ——

PEG: Go on, tell him.

HARRY: No, no. It's predictable. She sits at home all day feeding the dog and he's drugged up to the eyeballs to stop himself worrying about it.

MARTIN: Hoo Ray.

PEG: I don't think they're as bad as Malc says, do you?

MARTIN (*to* HARRY): Did you behave yourself? I see you combed your hair for the first time this weekend.

PEG: He didn't put a foot wrong. Clean hanky. After you Mrs Forbes, what a lovely lawn, and no I don't play golf Mr Forbes but I do watch television.

MARTIN: Revolting.

PEG (*jokey*): It was a very seemly affair.

HARRY (*to* PEG): You can talk. There was me stuck in the thing they call the 'lounge' with old bumbleguts on one side and the dancing horses on the other. And your mad mother going it like crazy in the kitchen. (*Enjoys.*) Independence, the widening perspectives of higher education, liberty. (*Ironic.*) Terrible stuff. It sounded straight bloody seditious to me. You'd never have known it was our simpering little Tania they were talking about.

PEG: Oh it makes me tired the way you attack people—really——

HARRY: Me? (*To* MARTIN) Which of us two do you think gave the impression of sweetness and tolerance—me in my demobs or our Boadicea here?

MARTIN: Hey, you know what though—I don't know whether they said, but Malc's got to see the vicar.

HARRY (*ignoring*): She'll never leave home. What's pathetic about that girl is the way she sits and takes it all right on the chin. Any other girl would have walked out years ago. She's got no guts.

PEG: Rubbish. You've never talked to her to know.

HARRY: She's a moaner. No action. (*To* MARTIN) What do you think of her?

MARTIN: She's all right. (*Reluctant.*) Nice legs.

PEG: What's that got to do with it?

HARRY: Have you noticed she's got no girlfriends? I find that pretty suspect.

PEG: You really are a clever dick aren't you? There she is—stuck at home because they won't give her the money to live away, up to her eyes in exams, struggling to find out what she really wants to do, and all you can do is despise her for it. She does very well, poor thing.

HARRY: Very well my arse. She simpers. Still it's not my business.

MARTIN: I don't reckon it'll go on.

PEG: You two make me so tired.

MARTIN: Well, it's all a bit thin isn't it? Old Malc getting all steamed up over his last two and so he rushes off and tries evangelism instead.

HARRY: What are you talking about?

MARTIN: Suburban girls: Malcolm is the answer to all your medieval problems. Widen your horizons as you play.

HARRY: Ah, my friend. That's the way you get devotion. Convert her to the cause and she'll never leave your side.

PEG: Typical man's way of looking at things: as if the whole thing was simply bringing women round to seeing the truth.

HARRY: That's right, isn't it?

PEG: She'll pull through whether she stays with Malc or not.

HARRY: Well she won't.

MARTIN: What?

HARRY: Stay with him.

MARTIN: But that's what I was trying to say. He's got to see the vicar.

HARRY: The who?

MARTIN: The vicar.

HARRY: What's he going to tell him?

MARTIN: What to do on the first night of your marriage.

HARRY: The mind boggles. We're talking about marriage already, are we? She didn't quite broach that one with us. Though I suppose . . .

MARTIN: He's in despair. He can't see a bleeding vicar.

PEG: Don't you think you two ought to mind your own business?

HARRY (*to* MARTIN): Ignore her. All this business has raised the female heckles in her. Any more gossip?

PEG: You wait. She knows she's got her dad's support.

HARRY: At a price.

MARTIN: God, she looks ill. Her face is all spotty and pasty. Huge bags under her eyes. The old lady's been going it five out of seven nights apparently.

PEG: Quite.

HARRY: Well we've done our bit. The dog and I see eye to eye on most fundamental issues.

MARTIN (*remembering*): Hey great. And listen to this. Quote of the week from the old lady—I bet *you* didn't get this one tonight—'After five years, the intimacies of marriage wear a bit thin. One might as well have a cup of tea.' Great.

HARRY: Pills, coils, loops—now tea. She really has got married life on the brain.

PEG: Why don't you two take it seriously? At least I spoke to her mother to try and help Tania a bit. (*To self*) It'll all have to happen slowly . . .

HARRY: Ah it's all such studied, over-scrutinized cock.

PEG: I think the old boy's not a bad stick.

HARRY: When he's awake. It was when she started telling me that the main influence on Tania's development was Sunday School that I stopped trying.

PEG: You never started.

HARRY: Mark my words, Pankhurst, before we know where we are we'll all be sitting round a wedding cake in the middle of some ghastly all-white methodist orgy.

PEG: What? You? No.

HARRY: Quite. I'm quite prepared to go along with a modicum of middle-class bullshit—but a church wedding? No.

MARTIN: I'd go down well there, wouldn't I?

HARRY: God, and that meal. (*Remembering.*) A bloody speech about every little bit of decayed cheese on the table. And as a special treat at the end of the meal she got out a tin of assorted biscuits. For every cream or chocolate one you get punished with eight thin-lipped, constipated Arrowroot ones. To summate an hour of dry lettuce—a heap of bloody protestant buscuits. Protestant biscuits.

PEG (*to* MARTIN): Is Malc all right? He hasn't rung for a bit.

MARTIN: Well he must know what——

HARRY (*grinding on*): Still, it's good to have all one's prejudices confirmed. Imagine how distressing it would have been going all the way over to Harrow and finding that you agreed with everything they said.

PEG (*to* MARTIN): Why do you two always pick girls with difficult parents? Do you think next time you could make a few enquiries first? (*Joke.*)

MARTIN: Maybe you're the difficult ones.

PEG (*to self*): I don't know, you know. I . . . (*musing*).

HARRY: What?

PEG: Starting up something new. Every step you make seems more difficult than the last. Having families.

HARRY (*not succeeding in interrupting the flow*): Here we go.

PEG: . . . and I don't think I understand this business of learning to let go of your children—you see . . .

HARRY: Or your husband. It's the emancipation of men I'm after.

MARTIN: Quite. Thousands of these girls reading books and no one to do the washing up. And they all go at it like rabbits, you know. Incredible.

PEG: They don't, do they? You don't carry on like that, do you?

HARRY: Sorry? Who doesn't interfere?

PEG: I think you have to make a serious attempt at making it work every time.

MARTIN: That's what he does, old Malc. And it *never works*.

HARRY (*looking at Peg. Winks*): Right. Take our word for it. (*For each other.*)

MARTIN (*to himself—detached*): Rabbits. Yep.

Scene Three

TANIA's *bedroom.* TANIA *working at desk.* MRS *making bed.*

MRS: You might have told me he was coming.

TANIA: I didn't know he was. It was as much a surprise to me as to you.

MRS: The fellow can't just walk in here and think he can get a meal, you know.

TANIA: He doesn't come expecting a meal—he came to see me.

MRS: And did he have the grace to say thank you when I did manage to find him a tin of something. I have enough trouble with——

TANIA: You were complaining so much he didn't have time to.

MRS: You're a liar—if I might say so, Tania—I hardly said a word, where I might well have done. The times you——

TANIA: Mum, can I get on with my work now?

MRS: But then, he's always like this, this friend of yours. When we ask him for eight he comes at nine, and when we don't ask him he troops in here as if he owns the place.

TANIA: He came to see——

MRS: It's so inconsiderate—to me and your father. There we were all quite——

TANIA: If you let him get on with the job of coming to see me he would not have time to be inconsiderate.

MRS: And do you think I can stand by and see him not being fed?

TANIA: Then what are you making all the fuss about?

MRS: Because it's time you learnt that people must be invited if you want me to get things ready for them.

TANIA: Who asked you to get anything ready? Round there, people eat whenever they want to eat.

MRS: Oh, yes, Tania, I know that it's second paradise over there. It just so happens that we have regular mealtimes here where the whole family meets for at least once in the day. That's the way it's always been and——

TANIA: For one of those little chats we're always having these days —or is it the food?

MRS: Don't you start that sort of nonsense. You can go to any other hotel any time you want. Or do it yourself.

TANIA: As if you'd let me touch a salt pot in that kitchen of yours! You would never leave me alone for a minute if I tried to boil an egg for Malc.

MRS: Well, it is my house, you know.

TANIA: Yes, well—he's more informal than that. And please let me get on with my work now.

MRS: Oh, I am sure he is. And he looks it. He thinks he can come here looking like a tramp.

TANIA: Mum, will you go away now. And I agree with everything you say. Yes, I am a liar—yes, he is a tramp. Please let me get on. I've got finals this summer.

MRS: That's all you do now, isn't it?—stuck in your books and mooning around after this—scruffy Jew of yours.
(*Pause.*)

TANIA: I don't want to argue.

MRS: Of course you don't, of course you don't. That's because you're afraid to think about it. Do you know about mixed marriages—do you? Parents from completely different backgrounds—it's so selfish for them to have children. They don't know where they are—who they are. They never forgive their parents for doing it, you know.

TANIA: No, Mum.

MRS: Would you take his name—you realize the difficulties it
would cause?

TANIA: Yes, Mum.

MRS. Yes, Mum—quite. They're neither one thing nor the other—
that's why. They go through life not knowing whether they
belonged to one or the other. Think of them at school.
You can imagine it. There was an article about it, only the
other day from a social worker—the children—it's not——

TANIA: Look, there's no question of——

MRS: Has he asked you to a synagogue? Has he?

TANIA: None of the family has anything to do with the religion.
Malcolm's never——

MRS: Does his brother go around with Jews?

TANIA: No—I don't know.

MRS: But they never leave it, you know. They never leave. He stays
a Jew. Why did he have to come bothering you? There
seem to be hundreds of little Jewish girls about nowadays.
I don't understand why you try to make everything so
awkward. There's——

TANIA: I can't stand this.

MRS: No, of course you can't. I happen to have had a little more
experience of life than you've had. (*Pause.*) Are you going to
stay with him?—Well, you can't. Where would you get
married for a start?

TANIA: Who's talking about marriage?

MRS: It would have to be in church. I've spoken to daddy about
that and he's adamant. We couldn't let you do anything else.
(*Pause.*) It would knock some sense into you if he found
someone else. I suppose he's been around, hasn't he?

TANIA: No.

MRS: What makes you so certain of that?

TANIA: I can't bear this. Can't you see I don't want to talk about
this now?
(*Pause.*)

MRS: Tania—I'm going to ask you something—he's 'been' with
you, hasn't he?

TANIA (*horrified*): I—I'm . . .

MRS: No, don't try and deny it. If daddy knew—he would throw

D   49

you out of the house. I shan't tell him, though. It doesn't
bear thinking about. In my house, too. That's what's
disgusting. And then you go around leaving your letters lying
all over the place. I've never seen such sloppy nonsense in
all my life. When people ask after you—I can scarcely talk
without thinking that——

TANIA: Why are you trying to make me feel guilty about it?

MRS: Oh, I am sure you don't feel guilty. You're quite brazen
about it. We can all see that. When I think of you a few years
ago—you'd've been horrified to know yourself as you are
now. The people you call your friends! What's wrong with
you?

TANIA: Leave me alone, please—it's got nothing to do with you.

MRS: Nothing to do with me? What happens when you're pregnant.
Who would you come running to, eh? You can't get rid of it
cleanly. We'd have to pay. You'll—Oh—I don't know. And
what will you say to your future husband—because *he* won't
marry you, you know. He saw you as easy kill. Sex. It's
all a game, is it? You can't know how easy it is to get pregnant
And you're the one we sent to university. The one who
couldn't get a job. That was the mistake we made. Letting
you go to university. Of course, we were only too happy
for you to go—we've always put your wishes first, haven't
we? And you—you're prepared to risk your whole career—
your future marriage, everything—for half an hour of
doubtful pleasure. He won't stay with you—then where will
you be? Just a silly little tart.

TANIA: Mum, Mum, Mum, Mum, I haven't done enough work.
Please go. (*Shouts.*) *Get out!*
(*Enter* MR.)

MR: What is going on here? Who do you think you're talking to
like that?

TANIA: She's driving me mad. I can't work, Dad.

MR: The noise is terrible. All I can hear is you screaming. The
noise must be going right down the road.

TANIA: Please go away and leave me alone.

MR: Well, really, Tania. I've never known you like you've been
this last few weeks.

TANIA: Not again.

MR: You were more sensible at school than you are now. We were all a lot happier. All I can say is that if it's to do with this friend of yours then it must stop. Now I've spoken.
(TANIA *is crying*.)

MRS: You've made her cry now. No one wanted to make you upset, Tania dear. Let me go and get you a cup of something.

TANIA: Please—both of you—just let me get on with this. We can talk about it when finals are over.

MRS: Yes, of course.

MR: Well, I had to be frank. I'm sorry if it sounded hard but then the truth sometimes is. I'm sorry, Tania. I didn't realize. I thought . . . (*to* MRS) Look, dear——

MRS: Well, I'm sure that's more than enough. I'll go and make some tea—— (*Exits.*)

TANIA: Yes, yes, yes, yes.

MR (*approaches* TANIA): I'm sorry dear. I didn't realize what was going on. I thought——

TANIA (*tears but snappy*): Yes, yes of course you did. I can't do it Dad. I can't open a book here without her coming in here and screaming at me or touching me.

MR: I'm sorry. I came up (*rueful smile*) because I couldn't work either. I was running over a few . . . (*waves to indicate 'papers, etc.'*) How *is* your work?
(*Pause—no answer.*)
You don't seem to talk about it much, mm? I was always interested in the——

TANIA (*belligerent*): It terrifies me. I'm a dud.

MR (*ignoring and musing*): You said once you'd invite me up to look around—see what you do. I'd've liked that.

TANIA (*bland*): Would you?

MR: You know when we agreed to you going there—well it was exciting, wasn't it? But your mother kept on about Mrs What's-her-name's girl—Glenda or Gwenda—that *she* had gone and so why not you—and . . .

TANIA: So why not me. Hopeless. Nothing's happened. It's all the same. Except my friends. (*Pause.*) Friend.

MR (*ponderous*): I think things *have* changed you know.

(TANIA *smiles at the plodding.*)
I'm afraid your mother's been—well you're *away* every
evening and she just sits and—well complains about it at us.
TANIA: Let's not talk about that. (*Change of tone.*) Every night I sit i
a vast empty white marble library, trying to work, and at
eleven a little lame porter comes and wakes me up, switches
out the lights and I walk down miles of corridors and halls to
come home to this. I watch the buses from the library windo
so I come home on *them* now. They're lighter.
MR: It's not true what your mother says, then?
TANIA: Which bit?
MR: You going round—I don't want to say it—You know she
thinks you've——
TANIA: O God—for the first time in my life I try and do something
different and for *him* it's not different enough and for *you* it's
foreign and filthy.
MR (*slow*): I just think in the long run, it's probably best to do
things that will finally, in the long run, cause the least
unpleasantness. All these arguments sometimes make me
wonder why we ever had a family. I think it's more difficult
than you think for us to accustom ourselves to you not being . .
(*Picks up one of* TANIA's *books.*)
TANIA (*snaps*): Put it down, Dad.
MR (*immediately withdraws his tentative warmth*): Sorry, dear.
Sorry. I——
TANIA: O I didn't mean that. Go on and look at it—look at it.
(*Tears again.*) 'Cell Physiology'. It's hopeless. I like it at the
Levins. I can't help that, can I, Dad?
MR (*putting book down and getting up to go*): I'm sorry dear.
TANIA (*oblivious*): I mind them being hauled into the argument. At
the moment they're very small.
MR (*going*): All right. Yes dear. (*Exits.*)
TANIA (*gets up*): Dad— (*goes to door*)—Dad. Don't go.
(*Comes back.*)

Scene Four

MALCOLM: Well, it's this really. Don't want to make it seem formal or anything but that—that provided all is O.K. when I get back from this Jersey field-trip then we'll probably be married. You know—the moment all this academic stuff is out of the way, eh?

PEG: Well, that's lovely, Malc.

HARRY: Well, well, well.

MARTIN (*shouts*): Best man. (*Arms outstretched.*)

PEG: We ought to have a drink on it, Harry.

HARRY: Quite.

MARTIN: I'm against it.

TANIA: How about you, Peg.

PEG: No, I think it's wonderful. What did your parents say about it?

TANIA: You don't think we told them before you, do you?

PEG: Well, I don't——

TANIA: It's agony at the moment. If they knew—I don't know what would happen.

PEG: Well, you ride it, Tania dear.

MARTIN (*shouts*): Worst man. (*Arms outstretched.*)
(*Re-enter* HARRY.)

HARRY: Hey, wait a minute, Peg, they haven't asked our permission.

PEG: No. It's the girl's parents you ask.

HARRY: Damn. I was just working out all the reasons why I could refuse.

MARTIN: Like what? She's a Jew.

TANIA: I'm not.

MARTIN: You're right. (*Quickfire deadpan.*)

HARRY: What about her parents?

MALCOLM: We were just saying. They presumably expect the real stuff. Daughter's hand in marriage—not lost a daughter but gained an idiot, etc., etc.

HARRY: Oh, gawd.

ALL: Cheers.

HARRY: Well, a marriage.

MARTIN: I'll invite all the yobboes, don't worry.

TANIA: Mum'll like that.

MALCOLM: She'll love it anyway.

TANIA: How did you two do it then?

PEG: Good Lord, yes. He said one day out of the blue: 'Hey, quick, let's go and get married. Sent me out to buy a ring; and when we got to the registry office the man said: 'Very nice, but where are the witnesses', and Harry said: 'Oh, we need witnesses do we?' 'So he runs out to the street stopping people with: 'Excuse me, would you like to witness a wedding?' One of them seemed to quite like the idea and so if you look at our certificate now it says: Witnessed by E. J. K. West. I seem to remember he was a very nice little man with a black moustache and a dog.

MARTIN (*points to* HARRY. *Speaking to* PEG): I knew you made a mistake somewhere. Look what you've got instead.

TANIA: Is ours going to be like that?

MALCOLM: No—we're having ours in a tent.

PEG: Has anything to be done?

HARRY: What do you mean?

MALCOLM: Well—when the time comes, I think we may have to say 'we're engaged' to keep them happy. And I think Tania would like—well, I suppose I do, too—well, we'd like a 'do' really. I don't see any way out of it to tell the truth.

PEG: Of course. Yes, that would be lovely.

HARRY: What, invite cards—the lot?

PEG: Don't start one of your stupid fits.

MALCOLM (*to* TANIA): Well.

MARTIN (*to* HARRY): Not all that rubbish.

HARRY: Shut up!

MALCOLM: I think it was reckoned that . . .

PEG: Of course. Yes.

HARRY: Christ!

MARTIN: Church? Confetti splurge?

PEG: Is there anything to be done for the moment, though?

MALCOLM: No, don't start knitting baby boots yet, Mum.

MARTIN: Huh!

PEG: Well, that makes me very happy.

HARRY: What, with a bleeding wedding on our hands—and just look at her.

MARTIN (*high-pitched maniacal exaggeration*): Look at her shoes. Look at her shoes. When have you ever seen shoes like that. Look at them. (*Etc., etc.*) Incredible shoes.

PEG: Leave her alone, will you, you lot.

TANIA: You know what Mum did when——

HARRY: Not again—the heartbreak stories.

MARTIN: You know what old Tania'll be like—Frank Sinatra in 'Cast a Giant Shadow'. Leaps out of his jeep, mobbed by thousands of hysterical dancing Israelis in Tel Aviv market place and he shouts across to Kirk Douglas, 'Don't leave me here—I'm ant-I-semitic'.

HARRY: You were saying, Tania?

MARTIN: Are you the only one allowed to interrupt in this place?

HARRY (*to* MARTIN): Read any good books lately? (*Hands him one.*) Scarper. (*He exits.*) Go on, Tania.

TANIA: Well, I don't want to hurt them. I can't help it the way it's all going on at the moment.

HARRY: Don't worry. You should have seen the bother we had with old Peg's mum. We survived, didn't we? (*Mock uneasiness.*) Didn't we?

MALCOLM: It'll be all right, won't it?

HARRY: Wedding cake, speeches, invite cards, new suit—Oh God. (*Still genial.*)

MALCOLM: We thought we'd tell you, eve of departure like and so on, so that it's sort of definite —I mean, kind of there you know.

HARRY: No.

MALCOLM: Never mind. I'm off tonight.

HARRY: That reminds me——

PEG (*pointed*): He's off tonight. (*Begins self-conscious exit.*)

HARRY (*quiet*): Might as well take the wine.

PEG: Leave it for them. (*She exits.*)

HARRY (*to* PEG): Any chance for a cup of tea?

TANIA: Are they pleased?

MALCOLM: I don't know really.

TANIA: Are you?

MALCOLM: No. (*Like 'No, dear' in digs scene.*)

TANIA: Is it all too early?

MALCOLM: What's 'too early' or 'too late'. These things don't happen by ordinance of Evelyn Home, you know. We could go on saying later for years.

TANIA: I don't know. Maybe—I've still got 'brambles'.

MALCOLM: That is 'umbilicals', which we're chopping, I hope. (*Enjoys it.*)

TANIA: I don't see what makes this one last and another one peter out.

MALCOLM: You don't mind me picking my ears.

TANIA: I do.

MALCOLM: Well, you're in for a lifetime of agony then, aren't you?

TANIA: But I could try and stop you.

MALCOLM: And you'd have as much chance as I have of getting you to throw away that bloody handbag.

TANIA (*serious*): Do you think that matters?

MALCOLM: What?

TANIA: Minding about things.

MALCOLM: Well, I suppose in a couple of years you'll be in a state of paranoia every time my fingers approach my head and I'll have a private collection of shiny black handbags that I'll get out every Sunday to pore over in hate—plunging knives and needles——

TANIA: You can't talk to me seriously any more.

MALCOLM: I don't want to go away.

TANIA: That's nice. They thought you were going to have your last one, didn't they?

MALCOLM (*annoyed, over-precision*): I don't know.

TANIA: That's what they wanted. Enlightened—attractive.

MALCOLM: And sexual dynamite—Oh, yes—don't start that again.

TANIA: They mind me wanting the marriage to be an occasion, don't they?

MALCOLM: I really don't know.

TANIA: Don't you want it to be?

MALCOLM: Yes, love.

TANIA: What?

MALCOLM: Well, we don't want the whole of Versailles along, do we?

TANIA: But a do is a do.

MALCOLM: What about your parents?

TANIA: What about them?

MALCOLM: What about them?

TANIA: They must come.

MALCOLM: Yes.

TANIA: What's the matter now?

MALCOLM: Well, look—they're doing their best to wreck it anyway. We don't do things their way. We do it our way.

TANIA (*insistent*): It's an occasion.

MALCOLM: Nothing changes with us just because we have a massed nosh-up.

TANIA: You can't run away after that.

MALCOLM: Pure bum. As if some bit of brass I buy from Woolies will either keep me loving or stop me clearing out.

TANIA: I don't understand you. (*Pause. Quietly.*) It won't be a brass one, will it?

MALCOLM: The statement 'Some bit of brass I buy from Woolies' was *a joke*. The following statement is deadly serious. If you think I'm going to have a marriage planned for me by some hypocritical methodist duchess—you're wrong. What's the matter?

TANIA: I want a hug.

MALCOLM: And while I remember it—you will come and see the folks while I'm in Jersey, won't you?

TANIA: Yes—I will.

MALCOLM: It means you can come away for the whole weekend and do some work without her getting her claws into you.

TANIA: But it's ghastly, Malc.

MALCOLM: You give in to her. You let her say these things, that's what gets me. No. Worse: Extramaritals is evil. This is because it makes you pregnant and if it doesn't it ought to. Extra-maritals make you sweat, have abortions, take drugs and squanders God's gifts to suburban battleaxes like the Mrs Forbes of our culture, thrashing it out in lifelong nuptial joy. And you worry. When in the last five years—twenty years can that woman——

TANIA: Please, Malc. This is your last evening. We won't see each other for a month now.

MALCOLM: Sorry.

TANIA: And don't run off after anybody else. You're not to have unconjugal lusts. Mum says that no man stays faithful for ever when he's away.

MALCOLM: Beats me how her man stays faithful for an *hour* when he's at *home*.

TANIA: Poor old dad.

MALCOLM: 'Dad'—with his saggy eyeballs—standing on his herbacious border paralysed with money troubles. And why's he making the money? So he can spent it when he gets home. And what's he going to do when he gets home? Take pills, mow the lawn, and have a really long-term *relaxed* worry. Or maybe go on holiday and walk up and down the quay *with ulcers* wondering when he can get himself back to that work that makes him all that money that gets him all that success that makes him so happy.

TANIA: He should never have married. He's a born bachelor.

MALCOLM: Or so that old lady can live as if she was in the back of a taxi all her life being driven to an affluent death with her eyes glued to the bloody meter.

TANIA: Why do you go on about them all the time? You can't talk about anything else.

MALCOLM: Christ. (*Panic.*) Hey, why are we getting married, anyway? I don't believe in it. All right for the kids, I suppose—most of them do all right out of it—except you.

TANIA: *You'd* be unbearably lonely if you didn't have anyone to spread your despair over for the rest of your life.

MALCOLM: Are you going to keep me company then?

TANIA: Shh, kiss me and say something loving.

MALCOLM: Something loving. (*Quietly.*)

TANIA: Stupid. (*Enjoying.*)

MALCOLM: I say that we'll be married and have a room with a massive bed in it and pin crappy pictures all over the door and cry because the bog won't work——

TANIA: And the kiddies? You'll like me when I'm pregnant.

MALCOLM: They'll be little brats with sticky knees, I'll teach the boys how to pee standing up and you'll sing to them when they bash each other up in the bathroom every night.

TANIA: And will you cook for me or will I cook for you?

MALCOLM: Lyons.

TANIA: Sundays as well?

MALCOLM (*gently*): Sunday will be hate Tania day.

TANIA: And can we be like we were at the weekend? It's never been like that before.

MALCOLM: How?

TANIA: All in the dark like moths.

Scene Five

Interior: a bar. On stage, ROBERT *and* TANIA.

ROBERT: Mummy said, what did I think was happening about the Caroline business and I said: 'I think it's on again'. Just like that. Straight out at her—no hanging about, and I think she was pretty shocked, you know. I came out with it. Bang. Just like that.

TANIA: Jolly good. So you are all settled with her, are you?

ROBERT: Well, I think she's a jolly presentable little girl, don't you?

TANIA: Yes.

ROBERT: Well, do you or don't you—I'm asking you.

TANIA: Yes. She's very nice.

ROBERT: That's what I thought. I was only asking, you know. I know Mummy was not too keen but I think she can be won over with a few flowers and stuff.

TANIA: Why bother?

ROBERT: I knew you'd say that. Well, she's a person like anyone else, isn't she? You talk about her as if she's a monster, and treat her like a pig. You ought to learn how to be on the right side of her.

TANIA: And look at you.

ROBERT: Why, what's the matter with me?

TANIA: Look how old you are and what you've achieved.

ROBERT: I think I've been pretty cool about life actually and it's paid off. I've bided my time on the sex thing, until I netted what I wanted, and all the while I've been looked after like a prince.

TANIA: That's sick.

ROBERT: What about you and your lover then?

TANIA: That's not funny, Robert.

ROBERT: Well, you behave like a stuck-up whore sometimes. It's so obvious that he lays you.

TANIA: I can't stand that word. Shut up.

ROBERT: What are you getting so acute about? You gone off it or something? Miss the old tickle while he's away. (*Laughs.*) You're such a little girl, aren't you? All this engagement nonsense.

TANIA: What's the matter with it?

ROBERT: About how no one must know this and no one must know that. It's pathetic.

TANIA: It's just so that we can tell them at a suitable moment, when I've finished my exams and have time to talk about it.

ROBERT: Hard luck. Too late. I told them this afternoon.

TANIA: You told them?

ROBERT: Well, they asked.

TANIA: But, Robert, that's ruined everything. Don't you see what will happen now?

ROBERT: Oh, don't exaggerate, Tanny, the whole thing would roll along as smoothly as hell, if you got your Jewboy to be a bit more polite to the folks.

TANIA: How can you talk like that?

ROBERT: Why, it's only colloquial.

TANIA: You're a bastard, Rob. You're an absolute bastard.

ROBERT: Well, well, well. So the secret is out of the bag. Now we'll have some fun.

TANIA: So what did they say? What did they say? Did you tell them that we've told Peg and Harry?

ROBERT: 'Told Peg and Harry'—oh—you're so weedy sometimes. They didn't say much. Mummy said the wedding had better be pretty soon and that she would have to get it announced officially. And then she said: 'I suppose if he had been a rich city Jew, we'd have considered a better match', which was quite funny, and what is terrible about you is the way family allegiance means absolutely nothing to you at all. That all you care about is Levin, Levin, Levin.

TANIA: What did you say in all this?

ROBERT: What I said was that it is such an obvious insult for you to go and see the damn people every day you can, trying like mad to show us you can't stand it here.

TANIA: I can't work at home, Robert, for Christ's sake.

ROBERT: Don't 'Christ's sake' me, Tanny, you are still fresh from confirmation classes and chats with the vicar. I suppose all that is overboard as well, is it?

TANIA: Leave me alone, Rob, please.

ROBERT: Well, I think you ought to cut out these flits to see them that's all. You don't even try to make any compromise, do you? If you made the ground a little softer before you trod on it, you wouldn't hurt your feet so much.

TANIA: Yes, I suppose so. But it wouldn't——

ROBERT: I mean, you don't even try to keep them happy. You set out to outrage them.

TANIA: I don't. I don't.

ROBERT: Well, make an effort to keep them happy. Skip seeing the Levins for a bit. Do a bit of help in the kitchen and she'll leave you alone to do what you want.

TANIA: Do you think so?

ROBERT: Of course. That's how I've played it all along, and I've always got what I want.

TANIA: All right, I'll give it a try.

ROBERT: They knew about the engagement business anyway, I reckon. All you want is for him to come and do the honours on old dad, like I did with Caroline's and that'll be that. It doesn't matter he's an odd berk.

TANIA: He's not odd. He's the gentlest . . .

ROBERT: Spare me, Tanny. Spare me the D. H. Lawrence, would you. You talk like an adolescent dream sometimes. That's what's so weak about you.

Scene Six

On the island of Jersey. Hotel lobby. Enter MALCOLM *and his friend* JIM. *They have entered to collect their mail.*

MALCOLM: She won't have written. You see. She never does over the weekend.

JIM: Don't know what you worry about. Not even the cat writes to me.

MALCOLM: No, no. She's written me.

JIM: Well, share it, will you.

MALCOLM (*reading*): But I——

JIM: All right, you can skip the fruity stuff. Oh, God—there's only the Telegraph this morning.

MALCOLM: Yes.

JIM: Give the appointments the once over. One day they'll offer ten thousand per annum for a totally useless scientist. Only idiots considered.

MALCOLM: Oh, God!

JIM: More troubles?

MALCOLM: Oh, God! Oh, God!

JIM: Well, share it.

MALCOM: I'll finish it first.

> (JIM *carries on reading his newspaper.*)

MALCOLM: No, no, no, no, no.

JIM: Come on then, Malc, spit it out.

MALCOLM: Wait. Hang on a bit.

JIM *carries on reading.*)

MALCOLM: I knew it. I knew it.

> (JIM *looks up, then returns. More silence.* MALCOLM *turns a page.* (JIM *watches him for a moment.*)

MALCOLM: The bastard.

> (JIM *ignores.*)

JIM: Hey, listen to this. Hey, listen. Listen.

MALCOLM (*not listening*): Yes.

JIM: Jersey wine, eight bob a bottle and it gives an address. What do you think?

MALCOLM: Yes.

JIM: That's fantastic. We could buy up a load of that and get completely whiffled on the last night.

MALCOLM (*still reading*): Yes. (*Pause.*) Damn her. Damn her.

JIM: No, I don't believe it. Malc—fantastic. Listen to this.

MALCOLM: For Christ's sake, Jim, let me read this first.

JIM: No, you won't believe this. This is the best news of the year.

MALCOLM: But it's always the best news of the year.

JIM: Well, listen: Malcolm Levin, B.Sc., and Tania Forbes under the engagement column.

MALCOLM: What a bad joker you are. Now just leave me alone.

JIM: Look. (*Stuffs it under his nose.*)

MALCOLM: Christ. They've done it.

JIM: But why didn't you tell me, Oswald.

MALCOLM: Quite simply because I didn't know, and if I did I wouldn't put it in there.

JIM: But——

MALCOLM: Now listen to this, Jim. It all ties up somehow. As far as I can penetrate those bleeding euphemisms, what she's trying to say is that we've got to compromise. Compromise. And that Robert's not such a bad bloke after all and a brother is a brother. I can't get to grips with what it's about. (*Reads 'Telegraph.'*) And how the hell did they know? Compromise!

JIM: Well, it looks very nice, Malc, I must say. Suits you.

MALCOLM: Who squealed first? Some of the time it looks as if Robert did and then others it's Tania. Why can't she write sentences?

JIM: Think it's time for a bit more bed, for me.

MALCOLM: And we've got to compromise. Did I want all this engagement rubbish? Not on your life. We've got it. Do I normally wear my one and only glorious Burton's suit when I go to dinner with people? As if it matters. I do now. And in reply I get fascist abuse. And what does she do? She sits there and blabs it all out to Robert, stinking little Fiona or whatever her name is, mum, dad, aunt, uncle, the vicar, the mayor. She's probably told them more than I know myself. And we've got to compromise. How can you match the daily enormities of that abusive old bag with this need to make the odd concession, Malcolm love. (*To the letter—*

shouts): When they call me a dirty Jew, it's you they're insulting, dear. I don't care.

JIM: Yeah, yeah, it's all very well for you to rave and roar about it but you don't look after old Tania very well, do you?

MALCOLM: Don't I?

JIM: No.

MALCOLM: Why—what don't I do?

JIM: You're always going on at her, hitting her.

MALCOLM: Well, I'm a ratty bloke.

JIM: Well, don't moan about her then. She's a bloody nice girl. Back to bed.

MALCOLM: What's that got to do with it?

JIM: You don't treat her right.

MALCOLM: Oh, I'll leave her to you and the Jersey wine freak-out. 'Treat her right.' No, I don't help Tania on with her coat and what's more—any spare belches, farts or rage I might release, are not preserved for an all-male audience of hot-rodding harries.

JIM: Well, why has she got to do all the compromising? It's about your turn now, isn't it? What's the matter with you?

MALCOLM: Look, Jim. Put a cake in it, will you? I could go on nosing the relevant bums for the next twenty years and short of becoming an insurance squirt with the right proportions of money, stupidity, god and impotence—it would make no difference at all. It's for Tania to move now. 'Been lovely having you, Mrs Forbes. So nice, bye-bye—mmm—lovely—always welcome—very nice, but I won't have another one, thank you very much.' (*Gestures dagger into* MRS.'S *back.*)

JIM: I predict you'll get nowhere. Tania doesn't want to break completely. She doesn't want someone like you.

MALCOLM: I can't stand it. It's so lousy. And that bloody 'Telegraph'; Let me have another look at the thing.

JIM: Here.

MALCOLM: Malcolm Levin, B.Sc. B.Sc. What does she care I'm B.Sc.? For six months she's been pretending I'm a maniac vivisectionist rabbi; and suddenly I'm a demure B.Sc. And does she help Tania get hers? Not on your life. It's been the symbol of her downfall. . . . The great hairy degenerate B.Sc.

64

and the suffering it brings with it. Oh, Christ, that's bad.
B.Sc. A bloody great B.Sc. up yours, Mrs Forbes.

Scene Seven

PEG/TANIA *phone-call. (Mrs Forbes calls out persistently during phone-call.)*

PEG: Hallo.
TANIA: Hallo, Peg.
PEG: Tania?
TANIA: Yes.
PEG: Oh, yes. How are you then?
TANIA: Oh, all right. You know.
PEG: You don't sound too cheerful.
TANIA: Well, I don't suppose I am.
PEG: No.
TANIA: And how are you?
PEG: Well, mid-term. No light in sight. I'm inundated. Well, I
    suppose you are too.
TANIA: Yes.
PEG: You doing that exam frightens *me*—I don't know how you
    do it!
TABIA: I don't think I do.
PEG: Well, things haven't helped much, have they?
TANIA: No. No they haven't.
PEG: If you do what you really want to do, then I'm sure things'll—
TANIA: But I don't know what I want to do.
PEG: Well, don't worry. I don't think I ever do really, you know.
TANIA: But it's nice when—well—
PEG: Will you be coming over some time soon then?
TANIA: I don't know—Robert said—I——
PEG: As you want. Malc'll be back soon anyway.
TANIA: Yes. Have you heard from him?
PEG: Oh—a postcard. He fulfils his minimum obligations quite
    well these days.

TANIA: Does he?

PEG: Don't you think?

(*Backstage sound of* MRS *calling out to* TANIA.)

TANIA: I don't know. (All right, I'll be down in a minute.) I never know what his obligations are.

PEG: I think that's the whole idea.

TANIA: Well, it doesn't make things any easier, does it?

PEG: But I don't think you ever know.

TANIA: Peg, I don't think I'm very good at cohabiting.

PEG: Pardon.

TANIA: I don't know. Some people you meet look all calm. Their faces look calm. They have things under control. I sometimes think I can't control anything.

PEG: But it takes twenty-five years to learn how to control *one* thing—so there's not much chance of——

TANIA: But some people at least look as if they eventually will.

PEG: It's just that everything's happened at once, isn't it? It gets distorted.

TANIA: What?

PEG: The exams. Your life doesn't depend on them.

(MRS *has called out a second time during the last speech.*)

TANIA: Pardon. (Oh, coming.) (*To* PEG): That's not what I'm supposed to believe. In ten days flat I've got to scribble down every single little thing I'm supposed to have ever learnt. It's turned everything into a performance. And I can't perform to order like that.

PEG: Has Malc been going on at you? Not that I'm allowed to ask.

TANIA: Not much.

PEG: Well, he moaned a good sight more than you do.

TANIA (*cheered*): Did he? Oh, did he? Well, I'll have to remember then, won't I?

PEG: Handy, isn't it? You know, trying to cope with those two— Martin as well, I mean—is like waiting for a wild boar to come tearing out of the maze at any moment.

TANIA: Do you?

PEG: Sorry?

TANIA: Do you wait? I mean did you? With—well—Harry I mean—Oh, sorry. (*Embarrassed that she's said that.*)

66

PEG (*tactfully ignores*): I don't really know. If you've made up your
    mind about the thing as a whole then I suppose you have to.
TANIA (*laughs*): But it's total subordination.
PEG: No, not really.
TANIA: I'm sorry, I shouldn't have——
PEG (*dreamily ignores*): No, I sometimes wonder. You know, I
    think young people make things move a lot quicker and easier
    than we ever did. I remember at the age of eighteen going
    to bed and lying awake in the dark for hours and hours
    fretting and worrying and crying over whether I would ever
    get married. Where would I ever find him. It never occurred
    to me to go out and look.
    (MRS *calls out again.*)
TANIA (*comforted*): Yes—well, everything's been so—I don't
    know—Christian, isn't it?
PEG: Well, I shouldn't start worrying about that now. Just clear a
    space for yourself to——
    (MRS *again.*)
TANIA: (Coming.) There's Mum again. Dammit. I must go, Peg.
    I'm sorry. Lovely talking to you. But I better not be——
    (Coming).
PEG: That's all right. Will you be coming over?
TANIA: Er look—I'll—It's difficult. I'll phone in the week some time.
PEG: All right then. Be seeing you then?
TANIA: Mum—hang on Peg—I'm on the phone at the moment,
    all right?—All right then. Er well, bye then. Thanks.
PEG: Bye.
TANIA: Oh, say hallo to Harry for me.
PEG: Oh, I shouldn't worry about him.
TANIA: Bye then.
PEG: Bye.

Scene Eight

TANIA *asleep in her bedroom. Suddenly the door opens and in flies*
MRS, *turns on light and starts talking instantly.* MRS *is wearing a*
dressing-gown, etc.

MRS: I can't sleep thinking about it. I can't sleep, Tania.

TANIA (*waking*): Oh, God, no.

MRS: Would any mother have stood up to what I have? Tell me
that. No, is the answer. She wouldn't. When would any
mother have sat back and watched when we have watched.

TANIA: Let me sleep. Let me sleep.

MRS: You've left the church, you never see your relatives, you come
home looking like a tramp. The way we see it, is that you've
been taken away and virtually raped. Do you think any parent
could stand all that, Tania? Do you think if we heard you
had been attacked while walking home through the park we
would say: 'Oh dear, never mind. That's the way young
people are.' We've tried to see your point of view. Everything
we've ever given you is thrown back in our faces. It's not so
much that——

TANIA: Go away now. Oh, go away.

MRS. And him, I'll tell you what he needs. A bucket of water
thrown over him. Can't you see it's just an infatuation? A
mad infatuation. He's just a lout. It amazes me that you can't
see that. That photograph you showed us of him in Jersey is
a nightmare. Horrifying. You are scarcely home any more.
Every possible moment of your life you are over there in
his digs in his sweaty bed. And you come back smelling of it all.
(TANIA *disappears under the covers.*)
Can't you see yourself, Tania? What you've brought yourself
to. You chose this. And daddy. You know he's ill. Every time
one of these things happens—he suffers. What I can't
understand is that you were so close, and the only
consideration you can show is to insult him. All right, I know
we're old and it's no disgrace to say so. His parents might
be young and tough—but I'm not. Daddy's not. You can't
go on treating us like that. And I'm not prepared to be
treated like dirt by him either. It's my view that you are a
pair of insolent arrogant young pups. It's we who have paid
for your education when you could have been earning money.
And you, you go on pursuing your own selfish ends, as if we
didn't exist. Your own parents. Tania love. You can remember
last year at Aunt Margaret's anniversary how everyone was
amazed at how nice you looked. You were a different person

68

in those days. I've lain awake at nights praying that you won't always be like this, you know. You don't have to get married to him yet. You could postpone it a bit. For your sake, Tania, you know. We could go away on holiday this summer, the way we used to. As a family. Together. And when we got back you could then see really whether it was worth going on with it. I think you'd soon see what had happened, you know. You could spend day after day on the beach, the way we used to. *And climbing the cliffs and going to see all the old places again. And that time you went water-skiing with Donald. I've never seen you enjoy yourself as much as you did that day. You're not feeling well now, are you? And him pushing you all the time. Pushing you to do what he wants to you do. A good long rest would make it better for all of us, you know. The sun—I'm sure it's going to be a good summer this year—the sea—and that white swimsuit of yours you haven't worn for goodness knows how long. You could wear that and, well—I think it's the only sensible thing to do you know—we could all be all right again— I'm sure Robert won't have gone—all of us . . . together. (TANIA *reads a letter* (*over speaker as she collects stuff together*).)

TANIA: Dear Mum and Dad,

    I have left home tonight. I am sorry I have done this but I have no other choice. I asked you to give us the money to let me go and stay in a university hall of residence for the next few weeks and you refused it. You know why I asked: it was because I cannot work at home. I asked you to leave all argument until after finals. Malcolm agreed not to come here and I agreed to say nothing about the future at all, but you have persisted in preventing me from doing my work. No matter what you think, I personally think that my work comes before all else. As a result of this, I have gone to stay with the Levins—who agree with me. They have given me Martin's bedroom and he has agreed to sleep in the front

---

*(*At this point freeze the scene on stage.* TANIA *sits up in bed in spotlight and takes over speech. She says it plainly. Unemotionally.*)

room. I tell you this so that you can understand what is going on. Tell dad I hope as much as I can, that this does not make his illness any worse and that he is not to worry. I will be all right with the Levins. I am sorry this has had to happen, but my exams must come first. As far as the marriage is concerned, the Levins have said that they will take on the organization of it, so you have nothing to bother about there.

Love, Tania.

P.S. My address in case you don't have it is: c/o Mr and Mrs Levin, 12 Portland Terrace, London, N.10.
Phone: Tudor double five O four.

ACT THREE

Scene One

HARRY/POLICEMAN *phone-call.* POLICEMAN *deadpan.* *Night-time.*

HARRY (*excessively ratty*): Hallo.

POLICEMAN: Oh—er—Hallo—Mr Levin? (*Pronounced it wrongly.*)

HARRY: Indeed.

POLICEMAN: Harrow Police Station here, Mr Levin. We've——

HARRY: What the hell do you want?

POLICEMAN: Well, I'm sorry to bother you like this but——

HARRY: So am I.

POLICEMAN: Pardon?

HARRY: I said, I'm sorry to be bothered.

POLICEMAN: Well, I'm very sorry, Mr Levin.

HARRY: That's where I came in.

POLICEMAN: Well, sir. This is just a routine enquiry. Well, that is to say we've got a Mr and Mrs Forbes here at the station.

HARRY: You lucky little people.

POLICEMAN: I understand that they are anxious about the safety of their daughter.

HARRY: What's the time, for God's sake.

POLICEMAN: Just after half-past two, sir.

HARRY: Mad—quite mad.

POLICEMAN: She asked us to phone you. That is to say the gentleman suggested that we——

HARRY: And what right did she have to do that, pray?

POLICEMAN: Well, Mr Levin—she informed us, rightly or wrongly, as the case may be, that their daughter is in fact reported missing and it is thought that you——

HARRY: Reported missing? Good God, man—as a young lady of twenty-one, as the case happens to be, she chose to accept an invitation to come and stay with us.

POLICEMAN: Is that in fact quite correct, sir?

HARRY: Quite correct, Yes.

POLICEMAN: Well, sir, the lady—well, the gentleman too I'd say—
are very upset and we rather suspected foul play of some sort,
sir.

HARRY: Well, you're wrong. Next.

POLICEMAN: Well, sir—

HARRY: Yes?

POLICEMAN: Er, could we have a word with the young lady herself,
sir?

HARRY: No.

POLICEMAN: I see, sir.

HARRY: You probably won't. The aforesaid young lady is in the
process of recuperating from shell-shock. She has already
slept well over fourteen hours a night for the last week and
having been roused myself, I have no intention of disturbing
her now. Was there anything else?

POLICEMAN: Well, there was one thing I have been asked to ascertain:
I wonder could you tell me, sir, whether the young lady is—
er—well, I mean your son *is* there, is he?

HARRY: What's that got to do with you?

POLICEMAN: Well, sir, I have been instructed to ask whether they—
as a couple—well, you know how it is—the lady is very
worried.

HARRY: Is she indeed?

POLICEMAN: Well, sir, I wonder could you tell me that?

HARRY: What?

POLICEMAN: Does she—I mean—well, have you got any daughters
yourself, sir?

HARRY: If you mean do they sleep together—I have no idea. And
I know of no way of finding out that isn't obscene.

POLICEMAN: I've been told they share a room, sir.

HARRY: Oh, really? Tell me more.

POLICEMAN: Well, sir. Put it like this. They've been here for two
hours now and they're driving me round the bend. Can't you
give me something to say to them?

HARRY: Ah, well, that's a different story. It's my help you want,
is it?

POLICEMAN: Well—

HARRY: No, no, I assure you I sympathize with your predicament.

I'd be only too happy to ease some of their weight from off
your back so long as I wasn't abetting their medieval pryings.
POLICEMAN: Well, look, sir. I would just like to ask—is the lady
fit and well, as we do have to make a report—I've got the
boss to keep happy as well, you know.
HARRY: Well, write this down in your little report that the lady,
Miss Tania Forbes, previously of 'Edenhurst', Laburnum
Grove, godhelpus, Harrow, Middlesex, is twice as happy as
she was last week and is now *bloody fine*. If there was anything
else you wanted to know, you can tell your Commanding
Officer that I answered the phone while still asleep and returned
to bed before you were able to complete your routine
enquiry. Goodnight.
(*Puts down phone.*)
POLICEMAN: Goodnight, sir, and thank—— (*Puts down phone.*)

Scene Two

Post-Policeman scene.

HARRY: So . . . (*Pause.*)
MALCOLM: I think he means he's going to tell a joke.
HARRY: *So,* one day the headmistress——
MARTIN: Which headmistress?
PEG: Do let him get on with it.
HARRY: The headmistress.
TANIA: He means my headmistress.
HARRY: I repeat, the headmistress.
MARTIN: What a bore.
HARRY: The headmistress finishes prayers, reads out the junior
netball results, chastises 5a's form captain for being seen
talking to men in school uniform.
MARTIN: School uniform *for men!*
HARRY: Seen talking to men in school uniform.
PEG: Who was in school uniform?

HARRY: Right, I am not going on.

TANIA: I don't mind if you don't.

HARRY (*turning on her*): You what?

TANIA: Sorry, I did not say anything, did I? (*Mock innocence.*)

MALCOLM: No, listen to this one, it's good.

HARRY: What do you mean, it's good? How do you know?

MALCOLM: No, I mean it's got good. Over the years.

PEG: Go on, dear.

HARRY: Last effort in the face of ridicule. The headmistress reaches the end of her announcements. (*To* PEG *who is going out of the room*): Where are you going?

PEG: No, don't mind me. I'm just going to have a look in the kitchen.

HARRY: But you like this one.

PEG: Don't worry, I'll hear it from outside.

HARRY: Right. Very last effort. She gets to the end of her announcements and she looks up at the vast sea of faces. All girls.

MARTIN: Great.

HARRY: And she says: 'Well, girls. I don't often have to talk to my girls like this, but owing to the increased frequency of—er—attacks in the Memorial Park and elsewhere—I'm afraid I shall have to do so today. I would just like to make it clear to you all that in this school, in this old and great school, this old, great and——

MARTIN: Come on, come on.

HARRY: 'This old, great and renowned school, let it be known amongst you——

MARTIN: He'd love to be headmistress.

HARRY: 'Let it be known amongst you that we want no girl amongst us who has lost her flower.' At which point a great sea of giggles and sniggers rises up from the floor. 'No,' she says, raising her right hand. 'This school takes its reputation from the dazzling careers of its inmates—not from the squalid beginnings of their offspring. You cannot afford, we can't afford to squander your careers on half-an-hour's doubtful pleasure.

TANIA: Good God! That sounds familiar.

HARRY: 'But remember, not only is this school old and great and

74

also renowned, but it is also—enlightened. I personally shall sit in my office for the next hour directly after this assembly, and any girl—I don't mind from which stream, from no matter which family circumstance, no matter how unfortunate—can come and see me there to talk over, to discuss any problem or worries you may have. This school is a big family. And in families people talk about things.'

MALCOLM: That's you, dear (*to* TANIA).

TANIA: Ssh, I'm listening.

PEG (*offstage*): You wait.

HARRY: So the headmistress sweeps off the stage; the floor of the hall rises into a mass of shufflings and gigglings and they all file off for contemplation of their problems. The Head, meanwhile, has settled herself down in her chair and sits waiting, expecting that at any minute Cynthia Squeedge and Fiona Fitzwell will be in for the pill—but no. Nothing. She sits and waits. Five minutes, ten minutes. Half an hour. Fifty-five minutes. Nothing. And then, just before the hour, just as she was about to ask the secretary to ring the bell, there was a knock at the door. 'Come in,' she says. And at about four feet below expectation, in creeps a small blotted mite of a girl, her face totally enshadowed by an enormous pair of brown glasses. 'Yes,' says Miss Greedledy, 'you want 1C's milk register, do you? Well, I am afraid it is still with——' 'No,' interrupts the girl, 'we came about what you said in assembly this morning, Miss Greedledy.' 'Really,' she replies warmly (as they say). 'Yes,' says the girl. You see, Miss Greedledy, we have discussed what you said this morning, and we thought we agreed with everything you said—but—but—how do you make it last half an hour?'

MARTIN: Pathetic.

PEG (*entering*): I do like that one.

TANIA: There's nothing funny about it, I can tell you.

HARRY: Oh, God.

TANIA: Look, you can talk of it as a joke. I can't.

MALCOLM: Take it easy, love.

HARRY: Anyway, have you done any work today?

MALCOLM: Listen to him. He's found someone else to nag.

75

MARTIN: You shouldn't have come here. He's far worse than your old lady.

PEG: True.

TANIA: True.

HARRY: I like that. Who answered the phone and with his own bare hands kept the whole of the Metropolitan Police Force from the door.

MALCOLM: I'll never get over that. They'll be sending time-bombs through the post soon.

MARTIN: Arsenic-sprayed Interflora.

HARRY: What a cheek they've got.

PEG: Does anybody want some more food?

HARRY (*mutter*): How do you make it last half an hour. Good joke, that.

TANIA: Doesn't he blow his own trumpet? All Levins blow their own trumpets.

MARTIN: I'll tell you something. Since she's come here, I can't call this place my home. She covers my bedroom with old knickers and I have to knock on every door in the house, in case I see her bare bum. A house full of lodgers.

TANIA: You didn't have to agree to my coming.

MARTIN: I didn't.

PEG: What about an exchange? You could go and stay with the Forbes's. They would like that, wouldn't they?

TANIA: He'd give them shingles on sight.

MARTIN: Fancy old pasty just walking out like that, though. Who would have thought it?

TANIA: Cheek.

PEG: It's more than you've ever done.

MARTIN: I have. When I was five. I got as far as the park and remembered there was the dirty old man with the stagnant nose in the cycle sheds and came running back.

MALCOLM: Just like you, love. Gets as far as the Levins's; remembers there's a dirty old man living there and goes racing back.

TANIA: I'm only going to get my typewriter.

MALCOLM: She just asks for trouble. First of all she sends them our address and now she starts creeping back. It's a wonder she can bear to be civil to them—and stop poking me.

76

HARRY: There's something chronically wrong with that girl—
    compulsive attraction for a bust-up. Good old romantic stuff:
    a bust-up's better than indifference.
PEG: I don't understand why you keep going on at her.
TANIA: Yes, leave me alone. I'm feeble.
PEG: You will come and see us when you're married, won't you?
HARRY: Like when they're broke and when they're lonely and when
    the boiler bursts because the oaf forgot to shut the flue and
    when the first child becomes psychologically maladjusted to
    living and the second psychologically maladjusted to the first
    —'come and see us'? Try stopping them.
TANIA: Do you know ...
MARTIN: She's going to try to speak again.
TANIA (*clips him*): Shut up (*not unfriendly*): Do you know I don't
    think old Dad ever knew how Mum went on at me. I never
    told him. And she certainly didn't.
PEG: She sounded as if she was running it single-handed.
HARRY (*almost sympathetic*): Oh the sad thing is the way people
    like them just make it tough for themselves. They're the ones
    who stand to lose. The old ones. Sitting there in their old
    age looking at pictures of the kids who hate them. Poor sods.
    If they're not back on bended knee to you by the time of the
    wedding ... then it'll be the first kid.
MALCOLM (*mutter*): It's got to happen first.
HARRY (*continuing*): It's bloody tragic, you know.
TANIA: Yes.
MALCOLM: Don't tell her that.
TANIA: What do you mean?
MARTIN: As worst man—at the big moment I'll be entitled to a
    smacker, won't I? God, I'll make it a good one.
HARRY: And as best man you're making all the arrangements for it,
    are you? Been to see the bride's parents? Ordered the flowers?
PEG: There's cards to be printed, a place to be booked, clothes
    to——
MARTIN: What a farce. No cuddles the night before, I hope.
MALCOLM: No, she'll sleep downstairs.
TANIA: I like the idea of staying apart the night before. It sort of
    gives you a short breathing-space to think about it all.

PEG: Yes—it'll make the morning seem special.

HARRY: What do you mean 'yes'. Where were you the night of your marriage, Mrs Levin?

PEG: Oh, dear, yes. The school air-raid shelter.

HARRY: A lot of breathing-space there. Oh, yes.

MARTIN: By the way—I forgot to say—that when you two are married, it'll be perfectly all right for you to (*gestures*).

MALCOLM: Shut up for a moment, will you, Mart?

MARTIN: Sir.

HARRY: Here, I don't know why you want to get married. It's not very nice, you know. All those bloody nappies and mewling and widdling and cocky little nits collecting bus numbers and pimply, leery louts like him and——

MALCOLM: You mean one smashed, disrupted family unit (*nodding to* TANIA), carefully nurturing another.

MARTIN: Do you reckon old man Forbes is still buttering his crumpet.

TANIA: You lot have demoralized me. I think I'm still at the pure love stage, I'm afraid.

MARTIN: God, it's going to be a good one.

TANIA: Keep him off me. Keep him off me.

HARRY: And no bride's parents now, I suppose. Mmmm?

TANIA: I—well, er——

MALCOLM: Well——

MARTIN: Our outside broadcast cameras are this minute trained on High Street, Gretna Green. Tell me, Gretna, would you——

HARRY: Do be quiet.

MARTIN: It's not me that's shouting. (*Yells at top of voice. Hands cupped to mouth.*)

MALCOLM (*to* TANIA): Don't worry love, we'll invite the dog.

TANIA: We will tell my parents, won't we?

MARTIN: Tell them you got the Jewish bit wrong and it's all right because you've just found out we're Black Muslims.

Scene Three

MRS *and* MR.

MRS: She'll be the loser. Don't you worry.

MR: Sorry? (*Equals 'Pardon'.*)

MRS: (*rhetorically*): Why do you think he singled out Tania? Tell me that.

MR: Well I'd've thought quite a few young men would approach the——

MRS: Oh he was quite calculating about it, you can be sure. Still— she'll do it our way or not at all.

MR (*gloomy rather than a retort*): She could be married already for all you or I know. (*More slowly*): Quite frankly—well—in the long run—I don't know that I'm in a position to say, but——

MRS: But then you never for one moment sit and think how we could help her to—make clear to her what she's doing when she goes off and (*gesture*).

MR: You know she stopped talking to me. She actually——

MRS: That's the least of our worries.

MR: I came in once and she didn't say a word to me from then until the next morning. Not even—simply——

MRS: Oh that was typical.

MR: I didn't do anything, did I? I can't think of anything that I did. There was no single moment when I—well we were always —I often think—do you remember that time there was me, Tania—no, you weren't there were you?

MRS: I think he really thought he could have his bread buttered on both sides, you know that.
(*Enter* ROBERT, *back from the office—coat and briefcase— interrupts* MR.)

ROBERT (*looking at watch*): Made it in thirty-five minutes twenty. (*Briefcase down.*) I think that's the record.

MRS: Quiet, Robert, your father's tired.

ROBERT: Any tea?

MR (*sudden to* ROBERT): Do *you* remember there was me, you, Tania and I think it must have been Uncle Jack and out-of-

the-blue we all decided to rush off—quite out-of-the-blue—
and——

MRS (*to* MR): Don't start on that nonsense. (*To* ROBERT): Why can't
you take tea at the office with all——

ROBERT: I did. I think. I forget now.

MRS: Aren't you going to take your coat off? (*To* ROBERT.)

MR: All right, my dear. (*Quietening her.*)

MRS: I can't think why he comes in and sits here in the lounge
when——

MR. Doctor came this afternoon.

ROBERT: Have you been at home then? (*To* MR.) You been feeling a
bit off colour have you?

MRS (*phoney stoic*): He came to see me.

ROBERT (*tactless*): What about?

MRS: Last night.

(*Silence—embarrassment.*)

ROBERT: Yes. (*Gets up.*)

MRS: Well don't you want to know what he said?

ROBERT: Yes. Well?

MRS: No, no no. He wasn't a lot of help. You know he never
really was an awful lot of use.

ROBERT (*amazed*): Who? Old Doctor Price? What do you mean? I
thought you were always saying—about Dad and him, how
he was the only——

MRS: Yes, yes, yes. I know all about that.

ROBERT: So what did he say?

MR: He said he could find no physical cause for—He said he
could find no physical cause for your mother's fit.
(*Embarrassed about 'fit'.*)

MRS: And that we've both been pushed to a point of nervous
exhaustion by Tania doing what——

MR (*bold*): No he didn't. He didn't say that. He said you had—well—
it was in your mind that——

MRS: What was in my mind? What are you talking about?

ROBERT: Come on, come on. Make your minds up then. What did
the old boy say?

MRS (*to* MR): What do you mean? In my mind? I want to sort this
out. You mean you thought——

80

MR: No, all I'm saying was that—he thought—I didn't—he thought you'd have to think about it all very carefully but if we could look after ourselves all right if you should want to take a short —a short—well, holiday if——

MRS: Exactly. As I've said before, I've had to manage this whole Tania business on my own. *I* have all the strain, and if she were to come back tomorrow—you'd be the one to benefit. You'd then go on and try and——

ROBERT: *I* wouldn't. If she want to clear off that's her lookout. Good luck to her. Huh.

MR (*meanwhile consoling to* MRS): All right, dear.

MRS (*to* MR): *You* don't care. I was the one who ever taught her anything. She looked to *me* for guidance. I fed her and kept her. Looked after her when she was ill. All you could do was spoil her. Anything she wanted to do was right. Small wonder she chose to behave like this.

MR: But when did I ever—(*stops*). Surely there was nothing wrong in——

MRS: And here you are saying she's all right now. Even when everyone knows she's wrong. I was always the one who corr——

MR: I'm not so sure everyone does know that. If she's happy—then maybe——

MRS: Well she isn't. You know that as well as I do. She was ill. Ill.

MR: Maybe. Yes. Maybe.

ROBERT: Oh she was, Dad. Ga-ga as well. (*Laughs.*)

MR: Yes, yes. I suppose so. And—that wasn't from anything *we* did, was it? I can't think that *I* was ever a reason for the kind of——

MRS: She was the happiest, when she was right here.

ROBERT: Look I want some tea.

MRS (*going out to get it*): She won't marry him. *I* can see that. The way he breathes over her. If she comes back just for a day or two, now that she's been away she'll see it clearly enough. And she'll have to come very soon if only to collect her books and typewriter.

MR: I can't talk to her.

ROBERT: Come on. Tea.

MRS: She won't marry her.

ROBERT (*to* MR *about* MRS): Is she all right? Did she sleep last night after all that?

MR (*distracted*): I don't know. I don't know.

ROBERT: I was wondering what it must be like living with people like those Levins. She must be like a fish out of water there. They can make her do absolutely anything they want, you know.

MR: Do you know what the doctor said? Old Price?

ROBERT: No. (*Bored—Pause.*) Rod is flogging his mini you know. I was thinking that if I could float a—— (*stops himself*).

MR: 'You don't own her, Mrs Forbes. She's not yours.' Old Price said that. Your mother had just said: 'Tania's our most treasured possession.' She's not yours. (*Mumble, mumble*).

ROBERT: Well. Beats me. She can't even conform to normal everyday civilities now.

MR: I suppose it *is* like watching a life's investment going to waste. Not even running at par. Your mother thinks that with a little pressure and this Malcolm business'll (*gestures*) break up. She looked ill, didn't she?

ROBERT: Which one?

MR: (*wry smile*) Yes, yes.

MRS (*from outside—subdued shriek*): She used to *live* here. (*Crash.*)

MR: Quick. Go and see what she's done now. Quick Rob. Go on lad.

ROBERT (*motionless*) Yes, yes, I'm going.

MR: Go on. Don't sit there.

ROBERT (*getting up*): All right, all right. (*Exits.*) You know the hall light's not working again? (*Pause*).

(*re-enter* ROBERT)

She's gone and dropped the milk tray. It's all right. It only had the milk on it. She's just clearing the—— (*clumsy gesture*).

MR: Well you could——

ROBERT: I'll go out tonight, I think. Yes. (*Looks around distractedly. Stands with back to audience, looking offstage at mother picking up broken milk bottle.*) Yes. Mmm.

(MR *sits in chair, puzzled and saddened.*)

(*Slow close.*)

82

Scene Four

MALCOLM: You've never seen a dog like their's. A great, blind, arthritic mongrel. That's all she does—look after Josie and 'entertain'. (*Imitates.*) Josie—another biscuit, Vicar? Josie—cup of tea, Josie?

MARTIN: Shut up, Malc—you're getting pathological.

MALCOLM: She must have been the sort of woman who woke up one one morning; collared some ineffectual, inhibited public school twerp and now——

MARTIN: How about switching it all off for a bit now, Malc, mmm? I've never met Mrs Forbes—I've heard it all before. Just leave it all alone.

MALCOLM: For Mrs Forbes—everything in the world is measurable: sex, lettuce leaves, number of plates wiped per week—it's all plottable on some huge graph——
(*Interrupted by angry* MARTIN.)

MARTIN: Right. Fine. All over now. You've been going on about her all evening now.

MALCOLM: Well I get—Christ—it's eleven o'clock—she's done it again.

MARTIN (*annoyed*): Enough for God's sake, Malc. What's the matter with you? Just try and keep some of these problems to yourself, will you? I don't want to know about it any more.

MALCOLM: She was supposed to have been back by five. She's got her hooks into her again.

MARTIN: Is that really so?

MALCOLM: No. Listen. Seriously. I know what's happened. She got there: collected what she wanted and was virtually physically prevented from leaving. She's staying the night and being brought hot chocolate by a penitent mother.

MARTIN: Well, that won't make any difference to anything.

MALCOLM: Don't talk nonsense. You don't know anything about this. Tania is swayed as easily as anything these days. She has gone through the last twenty years having every damn little decision and choice made for her. Where to buy a pen, when to go to the bog, where to go on holiday. Do you know —when she goes into a caff she can't even decide whether she wants a doughnut or an eclair and ends up in an anguish of guilt-ridden self-indulgence with a Chelsea bun.

MARTIN: Well, that's a fine bloody thing to say. Here she is in the throes of all this exam stuff, self-banishment and God knows what, and you——

MALCOLM: Oh, hell. Everyone knows what she needs except me and her.

MARTIN: Yeah, well who cares?

PEG (*entering backwards*): It's not in here—what colour again?

HARRY: Reddish.

PEG (*looks on shelves*): No, definitely not. You must have left it in school. Have you seen the moon tonight, you two? It is completely orange. Really. Go and have a look.

MARTIN: The wonderful world we live in, (*exits*) into which we are one day thrust; from which we must all one day depart.

PEG: Really—go and have a look, Malc.

MALCOLM: Yeah, yeah. She's done it again, Mum.

PEG: Please, Malcolm—no more. No more. We're busy. There's a lot of other things to be done tonight, you know. We've got two meetings to——

MALCOLM: You've given up caring about it, haven't you? You don't want this thing to happen either. And never have.

PEG: If you're going to start a scene like this—then have it with your father, not me.

MALCOLM: What a way to try and start a marriage: with as much support under your arse as a hot, plopping, bloody mud pool. (*Enter* MARTIN.)

MARTIN: Fantastic. What a thing. Why does it come up like that, Malc?

MALCOLM: I don't know. Oh, sod!

PEG: It's no use doing a sulk about it. (*Getting very annoyed.*)

MALCOLM: A fat lot of help—you've been. A sort of passive acceptance of her: tolerant and nice.

PEG: I don't know what it is you want from us, Malcolm. Just remember it's us who are putting her up so that she can get on with her work. If only you looked far enough to see—

84

we've given the pair of you a bit of space to move in. I'm not sure she knows how to stand on her own two feet, that girl. (*Furious.*)

MALCOLM: 'That girl.' (*Furious.*)

HARRY: What is it you expect from us, Malcolm? You can behave how and when you like with Tania—it makes no difference to us. Where it does make a difference is when you make demands on our behaviour towards you. Because she's supposed to be working, she hasn't touched a dishcloth since she's been here and we haven't asked her to. It was understood that she would get on with what she had to do. But on top of all the extra work involved, you start moaning at Peg and asking for yet more moral bloody support. We're putting the girl up—we're organizing a marriage for you and you sit here and start up one of your 'hard life' stories. It's a bloody cheek, that's all I can say. (*Pause—paces up and down.*) No one's saying anything against the girl, but she's got no guts. I don't know whether the pair of you know what it is you're trying to run. She's moved out of one dependent set-up straight into another without a thought for her independence. I should work out whether either of you are ready to cope with the demands you make on each other before making extra demands on us.

(*Enter* TANIA. MARTIN *cheering.*)

TANIA: Have you seen the moon?

MARTIN: Brilliant. Timing. Hooray. Well done.

MALCOLM: But you've come back.

PEG: Hallo, Tania.

TANIA: I've what?

MALCOLM: Come back.

TANIA: What's the matter?

MARTIN: He thought you'd done a bunk. (*Exit.*)

TANIA: He thought that, did he? Well.

(PEG *exits, followed soon by* HARRY.)

MALCOLM: No, Tania, love, I thought that—Oh, Jesus, I'm sorry, but you're so late.

TANIA: That's a fine thing to think I'd gone and done. Is that what you've been talking about? (*Looks around.*) Really, I got

what I wanted—left—met Alice in town as planned and
walked back from the station. Right?

MALCOLM: I'm sorry. I got worried. The research has been all
screwed up today or something. I don't know. (*Pause.*) Last
time you didn't come back, though, did you? (*Furious.*)

TANIA (*goes to exit*): So?

MALCOLM: And the next day you were telling me about dear
desolated mum.

TANIA: And so she is, Malc.

MALCOLM: But that doesn't give her the right to try and stop it all.
(*Yell.*)

TANIA: Why are you starting this now? I must go and do some
work now. I've come back, haven't I?

MALCOLM: For a bit.

TANIA: Look, Malc—it's not you that's had to change. You
wouldn't want to be separated from your family. A couple
of years ago there wasn't a Saturday morning I didn't go
out with Mum. Now look at it.

MALCOLM: I know that. I know that. But how much longer are
you going to think like that? In the long run it's a choice. We
run this thing on our terms. If they've made the choice to
behave like that towards us then they've made you choose.

TANIA: We've had this before. You talk about it all as if it's some
part-exchange deal. I've told you I can't bear seeing Dad
hurt like that; It's his face or something.

MALCOLM: And me?

TANIA: I don't know, I don't know. I can't think about all this now
It's only a week to go now, Malc. My degree.

MALCOLM: All right—do it their way. The minimum demand,
according to your mindless brother, we should compromise
with at the moment, is that we should delay it. Pure bum.

TANIA: Please, let's not argue about it now.

MALCOLM: What gets me is that you think that that would keep
them happy. You're never prepared to talk about it.
(*Beginning to shout.*) Delay it then. Go on, delay it. And see
them getting a second wind, in the 'Salvation of Tania'
campaign. Go home and listen to how I ruin your life. Every
night. Unload all your worries on to her loving shoulders

in that wonderfully encouraging compulsive way you have. 'Hallo, Mum, I'm tired. Hallo, Mum, I'm unhappy, overworked, ill, hungry, sterile, bullied—Mum, will you help me worry. Mum, will you please prey on my misfortunes.'

TANIA: Stop, stop—no more, Malc. Why do you torment me?

MALCOLM: 'Hallo, Mum—I'm neurotic—Mum, I don't like my work, Mum, please mother me'—'I'll look after you, dear.' (TANIA *groans and turns away*.)

MALCOLM: Going home for a month after your exams, are you? Mmmm?

TANIA: That's a fatuous bloody question and I'm not answering it. (*Hits him. Shrieks.*)

MALCOLM (*acted pause*): Hey, hey, an answer—a rejoinder—a counter-attack. The first ever. The highest temperature recorded since we set up our tracking station. (*Shouts.*) Oi, oi, Tania's just lost her virginity.

TANIA (*not unamused, but still hurt*): Oh, stop it. Sometimes you make me—I, well, I want to scream inside. I can't. (*She has to stop—silence for dry tears.*)

MALCOLM: Mother (*Inoffensive raspberry/vomit.*) Mother. (*Inoffensive raspberry/vomit.*)

TANIA: Have you got a hankie? (MALCOLM *takes out a handkerchief: spreads it across the whole of her face: all of it, and then holds her nose through it: she blows while he makes simultaneous blow burbles outside.*)

TANIA (*watching him*): There's never any need to go on like that. It doesn't do any good.

MALCOLM: Kiss me, then. (*She does.*)

TANIA: I want you, of course I do, but you must know I don't want them.

MALCOLM: Whatever they do or say?

TANIA: Yes, or—Oh, I don't know. I can't think straight about it with so much on my plate at the moment. I'm behind on my schedule again.

MALCOLM: But where's the doubt? It's them that want you to choose. All your dithering and doubts make them think they're backing a stayer.

TANIA: It's not so easy. It's not so easy.
MALCOLM: Well, hell, Tania.

Scene Five

London University.
Outside the building stands ROBERT, *clearly waiting for* TANIA *to finish the exam.*

TANIA (*not visibly pleased*): Hallo—what are you doing here?
ROBERT: I thought I'd come and meet you. That's all.
TANIA: Well, that's very nice. How did you know where to come?
ROBERT: I phoned the university.
TANIA: Mmmm. (*Awkwardness all round.*)
ROBERT: Well, how did it go?
TANIA: All right—not brilliant. I may have got a 2:1. It's all over
    now. The last exam of my life.
ROBERT: Yes—well—where are you going now?
TANIA: Back to see Malc.
ROBERT: Oh, do you want to go then?
TANIA: Well . . .
ROBERT: No, that's all right.
TANIA: No, let's go and have a sit somewhere for a bit then.
    Somehow you don't expect it to be sunny when you come out
    of an exam. I did better on this paper than I thought I would.
    That pleases me. London's all right, you know.
ROBERT: Well, how are you then, Tania?
TANIA: Well, fine—you know——
ROBERT: No, I mean about everything.
TANIA: Yes, yes. 'Everything's' all right. What do you want to
    know, Robert?
ROBERT: No, I was just wondering about you and Malcolm. What's
    happening and everything.
TANIA: Did mummy send you?

ROBERT: I came because I wanted to know how you were getting on.

TANIA: Thanks, Rob. Well, we're getting married soon.

ROBERT: Are you going to tell Mum and Dad?

TANIA: I would if I could....

ROBERT: Why, what's stopping you? Malcolm?

TANIA: No, no. I want to tell them but I can't. It's the way they've made it. I never wanted to leave home.

ROBERT: Look, Tania. I've got to go soon. Er—there was this (*taking out big envelope from snazzy briefcase*).

TANIA: Oh, I see—you didn't just come to see me then.

ROBERT: Yes, I did. I told Mum I was coming to see you and she said to give you this.

TANIA: What is it?

ROBERT: I don't know exactly. They've written a letter to go with it.

TANIA: Why should you do all their dirty work for them?

ROBERT (*embarrassed*): Yes, yes.

TANIA (*tearing envelope*): What's—oh, here (*takes out letter from parents while glancing back at the rest of the stuff in the envelope*). (*Reads.*) But this is fantastic. (*Laughs.*) They must have gone mad. When——

ROBERT: Well, what does it say?

TANIA: As if you don't know.

ROBERT: I don't.

TANIA: 'Here are all your personal documents. Robert has been instructed not to hand them over to you until he has obtained your signature on the affidavit.' Oh, well, you mucked that up, didn't you?

ROBERT: Yes.

TANIA (*holding them out of his reach suddenly*): Well, you'd look a right nit if I didn't sign this thing now, wouldn't you?

ROBERT: Yes, I suppose so.

TANIA: Actually in the long run I think it's more insulting for me to give it to them than to refuse. Here it is. I haven't quite got the cheek to call it Tania Levin. (*She signs and rummages through documents.*) As if I care about my 'throwing-the-rounders ball' certificate from—hey, where's my birth certificate? (*Rummages.*)

ROBERT: Well——

TANIA: Don't tell me there's some rubbish over that as well. (*Pause.*) Eh?

ROBERT: They said that that is *their* property. (*Squirming.*)

TANIA: But what if I apply for a——

ROBERT: Look, Tanny, I didn't want to do all this. I came to see you but Mummy collared me.

TANIA: Oh, sure, you never were exactly gutty, were you?

ROBERT (*blurt*): And they've disinherited you.

TANIA: I can't keep up, I really can't. I'm disinherited? Disinherited of what?

ROBERT: Your money or something.

TANIA: But I didn't have any money.

ROBERT: Of course you did. They had hundreds put away for you, for when you—well, got married or something.

TANIA: What are they doing that for? Keeping it out of the hands of those unscrupulous friends of mine. This is unbelieve——

ROBERT: Actually—to tell the truth—I think that Mummy thinks that Malcolm was after your money all along.

TANIA (*starts laughing*): But Rob, this is mad. I don't know, I don't care. 'Cutting me off for marrying beneath me.' He'll have his Ph.D. in—Oh, it's all so silly. Plain silly. They can keep their legacies and heirlooms. I won't be running my life based on that. And do you know what? When I came home last. That time. (I didn't connect, did I?) that last time— the ruby brooch mad Aunt Charlotte gave me was locked in Mum's dresser. How could they have spent so much time thinking about all——

ROBERT: It was a lot of money, Tania; you've thrown it all away with the way—Oh, I don't know either.

TANIA (*laughs at him*): Oh, you fool, Rob.

ROBERT: Why don't you take it seriously?

TANIA: Oh, really. You come and meet me like a little schoolboy meeting his mother—hand me over what are supposed to be the—well, what do they think it all is—the foundations of a contented life. You're telling me to be serious. That's it now, Rob. There's nothing left.

ROBERT: Do you care about it?

TANIA: I care. I care. What upsets me on reading this is that Mum along with you and Dad sat down one day this week and said: 'Well, she doesn't want our blessing—so she shan't have our money.' It's the premeditation of it—not the money that upsets me.

ROBERT: You're talking rubbish again.

(*Pause.*)

TANIA: It's not nice seeing you again, Robert.

ROBERT: I don't suppose it is.

TANIA: Tell them they can have their money. I would never have taken it from them anyway. I'd've been accused of a lifetime's ingratitude. Tell them I'm getting married. That makes me happy. How it happens doesn't really matter now.

ROBERT: No doubts?

TANIA: Why do you ask?

ROBERT: No, no, no, no. Well, I mean I have had doubts with Caroline.

TANIA: Have you?

ROBERT: Well, she's not brilliant company, is she? I was thinking that maybe a lifetime might be rather dull. Those sort of doubts.

TANIA (*laughs*): It won't be dull. It's all the battles that would make me doubt. If I did. Keeping everything at bay.

ROBERT: I've never argued once with Caroline—about anything.
(*Regretful, not superior.*)

TANIA: It's the idea of keeping everything off the ground at the same time. Him, me, kids, friends, all above the ground—all at the same time, so that nobody gets bumped. That frightens me. Though Peg manages even in that menagerie. I'd love to be calm. To be able to manage things.

ROBERT: Been all right living with them, has it?

TANIA: Yes, it's like a kids' playground, the whole time. No one stops shouting.

ROBERT: But still better than home?

TANIA (*dodges the irony*): Nowhere's right for me at the moment, till I've made a place of my own.

ROBERT: I'm moving into a flat soon.

TANIA: Are you?

ROBERT: Well, soon—probably. (*Total weediness.*)

91

TANIA: I've never lived on my own anywhere. I don't suppose I ever will now. Really on my own, I mean——

ROBERT: I don't suppose it matters.

TANIA (*contradicts*): I don't know. Sometimes I think all I do is drift. Move from one thing to another with some vague idea in my mind that it might just possibly be right. I'd have liked some bloody advice—not a cancelled will.

ROBERT: University all over too, eh?

TANIA: That seems daft, too. I've scarcely done a thing there, met nobody I really ever want to see much of in the future. I enjoyed myself more at school. At least we *laughed* at things there. I don't know what I expected, but sometimes I think I might just as well have had a good sleep. I might have finished my exam today and pottered quietly off home just like I used to: make Mum the tea, sat and watched telly, and pottered off to bed.

ROBERT: Well, you potter off to little hubby now.

TANIA: If it happens quick like this, we'll be able to start properly and freely, I want that.

ROBERT: *Do* you love him then?

TANIA: I want to make him happy. That's all I know. You know— a few years ago I'd have been really appalled and frightened at what I've done. What I do now.

ROBERT: Look, I must go now, Tanny. You will come and see me when you're all fixed up, won't you? I mean—just because you have a row with the parents doesn't mean we never see anything of each other, does it?

TANIA: Of course we will. Well—*you* come and see *us*. We're going to have a flat, too.

ROBERT: Well—bye then.

TANIA: But you didn't tell me about the Caroline business or anything.

ROBERT: Oh, next time then.

TANIA: And I didn't tell you—I'm pregnant.

ROBERT: Are you?

TANIA: I might be.

ROBERT: Well, are you or aren't you?

TANIA: Sort of. (*Teasing, smiling.*)

ROBERT: No, look, tell me one way or the other.

TANIA: I'm happy to *think* I am. It makes me want it all as quick as possible. Plonk—right in the middle—from the start. As far as I'm concerned the do is for a baby. Well, three people in the future.

ROBERT: I don't know whether you're having me on or not. Look—er—if you're pregnant you've got nothing to worry about because—well, if you're not you've—er—got nothing to worry about.

TANIA: It's nice, isn't it?

ROBERT: I don't know. I must go. I don't understand anyway. Look, do you want me to tell Mum about when the wedding is.

TANIA: But *you* don't know when it is either.

ROBERT: No.

TANIA: No. (*Pause.*) Tell them it's soon—or tell them what you want. It doesn't make any difference now, does it? They've made me choose. It doesn't matter when. It doesn't matter whether I do or don't. I'm just trying to begin and——

ROBERT: Don't worry. I'll tell you this, Tania. Watching them and you has . . . well, anyway, I'll see you again, won't I?

TANIA: Yes, bye-bye, then, Rob. All the best.

ROBERT: Bye and send me what degree you get. I'd like to know and everything.

TANIA: Yes, of course.